William Jefferson Lhamon

Missionary Fields and Forces of the Disciples of Christ

William Jefferson Lhamon

Missionary Fields and Forces of the Disciples of Christ

ISBN/EAN: 9783337779825

Printed in Europe, USA, Canada, Australia, Japan

Cover: Foto ©Lupo / pixelio.de

More available books at **www.hansebooks.com**

Hand-book Series for the
Bethany C. E. Reading Courses

✠

Missionary Fields and Forces

OF THE DISCIPLES OF CHRIST.

BY

W. J. LHAMON,

DIRECTOR OF STUDY OF MISSIONS IN THE
BETHANY C. E. READING COURSES.

✠

Bethany C. E. Company
798 Republic Street
Cleveland, Ohio

The National Convention of the Disciples of Christ, held in Springfield, Illinois, October 16-23, 1896, adopted the following recommendations:

"1. That this convention approve the idea of adding, within certain limits, the educational feature to the Christian Endeavor Societies among us. This added educational feature shall include helps for the systematic reading of the Bible, a selected course of reading concerning missions in general, and our own missions in particular, and thorough instruction as to the origin, the principles, and the history of our own movement for the restoration of New Testament Christianity.

"2. That this convention approve of the purpose to provide a series of hand-books for our young people covering the fields not already satisfactorily covered."

In harmony with this action three courses of reading are being planned and a hand-book, introductory to each course, has been prepared. This little volume is the second hand-book in the study Missions.

CONTENTS.

	PAGE
I. The Primitive Gospel in Modern Missions....	7
II. Foreign Christian Missionary Society................	18
III., Our Fields and Forces in India....	21
IV. Our Fields and Forces in China...	32
V. Our Fields and Forces in Japan.......	40
VI. Our Fields and Forces in Turkey....................	46
VII. Our Fields and Forces in Scandinavia..............	50
VIII. Our Fields and Forces in England...........	53
IX. Our Fields and Forces in Africa....................	56
X. Our Medical Missions...............................	62
XI. Christian Woman's Board of Missions..............	68
XII. American Christian Missionary Society	80
XIII. Board of Negro Education and Evangelization......	96
XIV. Church Extension...................................	105
XV. Board of Ministerial Relief..........................	109
XVI. The Educational Board.............................	112
XVII. Religious Conditions in England.............	114
XVIII. Hinduism.............	118
XIX. Confucianism..................................	126
XX. Buddhism....................	133
XXI. Mohammedanism	142
Appendix.....…………. ....….	147

Missionary Fields and Forces

OF THE DISCIPLES OF CHRIST.

CHAPTER I.

INTRODUCTORY.

THE PRIMITIVE GOSPEL IN MODERN MISSIONS.

1. The Gospel is a revelation. Theology is an invention. It is the office of the followers of Jesus to proclaim the former. The commission of the Master does not include the latter. Christ is perfection, and his work a completion. He is God's last and best word to us; he is "the fullness of him that filleth all in all;" he is "man at his climax;" he is "the moral miracle of history;" he is "the surprise of the ages;" he is "the Word made flesh," and —"We have seen his glory, the glory as of the only begotten of the Father, full of grace and truth."

He said to Thomas: "He that hath seen me hath seen the Father; and how sayest thou then, show us the Father?" His love is God's love; his forgiveness, God's forgiveness; his justice, God's justice; his Brotherhood, God's Fatherhood.   He is to be received as the fullness of the Father's will toward men and life in men, and his matchless manhood towering into Godhood should stand to us forever as a warning against the futile search for further revelation.   When therefore he, clothed in the victory of his resurrection from the dead, said, "Go teach all nations, baptizing them in the name of the Father and of the Son and of the Holy Spirit," he gave the message in its fullness which he intended his followers forever to declare.

And that is precisely what they did declare. On the day of Pentecost (Acts ii), the Apostle Peter, moved by the Holy Spirit, testified of Jesus that God had raised him from the dead and made him both Lord and Christ.   His sermon carried conviction to three thousand souls, thus in the first presentation of the Gospel showing the perfect work of the Gospel.   Later other thousands were added; later still, in the home of Cornelius (Acts x), Peter again testified of Christ, and there were gathered into the church the first fruits of the Gentile world.

2.   The work begun by Peter was caught up by Paul, and his cry rang throughout the pagan, Roman world, "I am not ashamed of

the Gospel of Christ for it is the power of God unto salvation to every one that believeth.'' To the Corinthians he said: '' I determined to know nothing among you but Christ and him crucified.'' To the Galatians he said: ''God forbid that I should glory save in the cross of Christ, by whom the world is crucified unto me and I unto the world.'' A chain of churches marked the pathway of this man, and the fires of his faith burned to the water's edge far along the shores of Asia, Greece, and Italy.

3. The book of Acts is the history of the first church and its marvelous missionary achievements. In it there is no dogmatic theology, and the supposed finding of dogmas and counter dogmas there has been ''the heaviest cross the risen Christ has had to bear.'' From the Apostle Paul's standpoint there is no '' Pauline theology,'' but Christ is all and in all. Nothing could have been more repugnant to his radiant and loyal soul than the accusation against him of a distinctive or divisive system of teaching.

It may almost be said that in proportion as the church became speculative she ceased to be evangelistic, and that in proportion as she permitted systems of thought, however true or false, to usurp the place in her work of the

Savior himself her evangelistic efforts were misdirected and enfeebled.

4.   Since the reformation the trend of Protestant teaching has been more and more away from creeds to Christ, and from theories about the Gospel to the facts of the Gospel.   Correspondingly, there has come a revival of interest in world-wide evangelization, coupled with evident signs of God's pleasure as shown in the redemption of great multitudes in many lands, and with glowing promise of the triumph of the kingdom of Christ in all lands.

5.   It has been given to the people known as Christians, or Disciples of Christ, to see clearly the futility of the dogmatizing tendency, and boldly to declare the sufficiency of the Scriptures as a statement of faith and rule of life.   Concerning doctrines we have said, "Where the Scriptures speak, we speak; and where they are silent, we are silent." This position puts us immediately in the very forefront of the great Protestant movement of the last four centuries, for it brings us directly back to the person and the office of the Lord Jesus Christ, and causes us to see that Christianity consists in our personal loyalty to his personal Lordship; that our only confession of faith should be an expression of his supreme

claim, namely that he is the Son of God and the Savior of the world; and that for our style of life no further laws or by-laws are needed than conformity to his style of life.

6.   While we were thus led to take the ultimate step in the Protestant movement, we were forced into a seeming antagonism to Protestantism itself, but really only into a protest against its incompleteness and fragmentariness. Luther said of Savonarola: "Some theological mud still clings to the feet of this holy man; but he lives in blessedness and Christ has canonized him." Just so, in all charity, we have thought of Luther himself, and of Calvin, and many another holy man, and of the bodies wherein they stand as representatives.

7.   Furthermore; the position assumed by us with regard to Christ and the Bible led us by necessity to advocate the original, normal unity of the people of Christ in the church of Christ. We saw clearly that the Savior is one and that his church should be one, and that if the New Testament presents the original, normal form of the relationship of Christ's followers one to another, denominationalism, being a radical departure from it, must be abnormal. We were constrained therefore to plead for the unity of all believers in the one

supreme object of their belief, and to empha-
size in our teaching the principle that seems
as clear to us as a mathematical axiom, namely
that all Christians can and should unite in
Christ.

Briefly, the position assumed by the foremost of present-day Protestants is this:

a.   Faith in Christ the only creed.

b.   Loyalty to Christ the only code of
conduct.

c.   Unity in Christ the ideal of organized
discipleship.

8.   The vitality of this position has been
demonstrated in our own land.   From a little
handful in the thirties we have grown to a great
multitude in the nineties.   During his life time
Alexander Campbell saw the movement draw
to its embrace a quarter of a million of people.
He died in 1866.   The ten years from that
time to our national centennial brought us
another 100,000.   In 1886 there were 650,000.
In 1896 above 1,000,000.   Our growth is one of
the surprises of the religious census from year
to year, and while others are seeking to account
for it in various ways we believe it is due to the
simplicity and power of the New Testament
position we have assumed, and to God's blessing resting upon us in our presentation of

Christ as Christ.   We are providentially placed in the very heart of the greatest nation on earth, and the genius of our New Testament position and movement is in admirable keeping with the genius of our nation, moulded as it is by the same book however unconsciously into democratic modes of thought and government.   From this central position, doctrinally as regards the Bible, geographically as regards our nation, God is thrusting us forth to a mighty work.   Let us pray that he may yet lay his hand upon us more heavily than he has ever done, and that he may make us a leaven among the millions of our native land while he makes us a conquering power to multiplied millions in other lands.

9.   Our work in foreign countries has not been established long enough to admit of comparison with missions that are well nigh a century old, but we have made a satisfactory beginning, as the pages of this book will show. We have laid foundations upon which there may be built "great things for God." We have many reasons to expect "great things from God."

Chief among these is the tendency of missionaries among pagan peoples to revert to the Gospel in its New Testament simplicity, and their experience thereupon of finding it clothed in its primitive, apostolic power. Invariably the name first exalted by missionaries is the name of Christ; the truth first impressed is the truth of his mediatorship as the Son of God and the Savior of men ; the motive first presented is the motive of God's love as shown in the gift of Christ, and incarnate in Christ; the book first translated is one of the four Gospels; then the New Testament; lastly the whole Bible ; the code of conduct first imposed upon new born believers is the golden rule and the sermon on the mount; while as the crown of all missionary teaching there is the forgiveness of sins and the salvation of the soul.   Now all this is thoroughly primitive and it is admirably effective.   Upon this Pentecostal presentation of Christ modern Pentecosts have been numerous in foreign fields.

10.   A recent able writer on missions affirms quite positively that "The same ethical and religious phenomena are being produced by the preaching of Jesus Christ as the Savior of men in the nineteenth century as in the first century.   The most solemn, and apart from the Gospel, the most crushing and dismaying facts are turned into grounds of joy and awaken thoughts of triumph.   The judgment of the

holy and righteous God, the sense of sin, the approach of death are transmuted in their significance for the human heart.   The dawn of faith, the quickening of conscience, the inflow of joy, the outflow of love, the experience of moral energy—these are the permanent characteristics of the Christian religion.   All these are effects which everywhere follow upon the preaching of the name of Jesus Christ.   That this preaching is conducted in various languages, or that there are differences of standpoint on many matters more or less important amongst the preachers of the Gospel does not destroy the identity of the message which they have presented through all the centuries and throughout the world.   The words of Jesus and his apostles come home to them with an authority before which they bow.   They universally find in Holy writ the fittest expression of their own thoughts, and the clearest descriptions of their own experience in relation to God and eternal life.''

11.   We have therefore in the mission fields of many lands indisputable proof of the power of the Gospel in its Pentecostal simplicity and its New Testament presentation.   Its light is not dimmed by increasing centuries, nor its efficacy diminished by its transmission from people to

people. In all ages and among all nations Christ when presented as he presents himself becomes the supreme object of faith, of love and of loyalty; his name rises above every name; his creed proves its sufficiency and efficiency to the founding, the furthering, and perfecting of churches and schools and Christian communities; his life becomes the ideal and the model of that "newness of life" to which his believing ones are invariably committed. Everywhere and always it is Christ that convinces, convicts, converts, forgives, inspires, completes, and so redeems.

12. The missionary who goes out with the Bible in his hand and the Holy Spirit in his heart has the whole power of truth and secret of success of the apostolic day. This equipment, being found sufficient in foreign lands, is reacting upon the churches of our home lands in favor of greater simplicity, less rivalry, larger charity, scriptural against speculative teaching, practical piety, and Christian union.

13. The people to whom it is given to see these things most clearly, and who therefore stand in the very vanguard of the Christward, Protestant movements of the age, should be among the first in missionary enthusiasm and

achievement.   Let such a people be as true to the spirit of Christ as they are to the recorded teachings of Christ and nothing on earth can stay them from a majestic influence of world-wide extent.   If responsibility is in proportion to ability a great burden rests upon any people that assumes so to receive and represent Christ.   The Apostle Paul felt that the Gospel was committed to him in trust, and that he was therefore a debtor both to the Greek and the barbarian, both to the wise and to the unwise.   The Gospel never ends with its blessings to the saved, but through the saved it reaches on still to the unsaved, and so in widening circles it seeks to encompass " every creature."

It is our humble trust that this hand-book, while setting forth with the kindly aid of other pens than that of the author a concise view of our missionary fields and forces, may be at the same time an inspiration to its readers to work and to pray for the furthering of our dear Redeemer's kingdom in all the earth.

———

QUESTIONS: 1. Wherein is the Gospel distinct from theology? 2. Which are we commanded to teach? 3. How does the Son Reveal the Father? 4. What was Christ's commission after his resurrection? 5. How is Paul's work related to Peter's? 6. What New Testament book gives the history of the first church? 7. What is the trend of Protestant teaching? 8. Name three distinctive points in our doctrinal position. 9. Where does this position rank us among Protestants? 10. What is our providential position geographically? 11. What is the doctrinal tendency of missionaries among pagan peoples? 12. What is the effect of the Gospel to-day as compared with its earliest presentation? 13. What does our doctrinal position demand of us as regards missionary effort? 14. How did the apostle Paul feel that the Gospel was committed to him?

CHAPTER II.

FOREIGN CHRISTIAN MISSIONARY SOCIETY.

1. Organized October 21st, 1875, at Louisville, Ky. Its first officers were: President, Isaac Errett; Corresponding Secretary, Robert Moffett; Treasurer, W. S. Dickinson. Its officers for the current year are: President, Chas. Lois Loos; Corresponding Secretary, A. McLean; Treasurer, F. M. Rains.

In addition to these officers there are five vice-presidents, and the whole body of officers constitutes the Executive Committee, to which are delegated all the powers of the Board of Managers during intervals of the Board meetings.

2. The object of the society, as stated in Article II of the Constitution, is "To make disciples of all nations and to teach them to observe all things whatsoever Christ commanded."

According to Article III of the Constitution the society is composed of Life Directors, Life Members, Annual Members, and representatives of churches, Sunday-schools, Sunday-school classes, and missionary associations.

3. At present the society has 7 missions and 103 stations and out-stations. These are the Japan mission with 5 stations; the China mission with 5 stations; the India mission with 4 stations; the Turkish mission with 3 stations; the Scandinavian mission with 27 stations; the English mission with 14 stations; and the African mission with 1 station.

4. The society is supporting 162 workers, 76 of whom are native helpers. The force in India consists of 21 missionaries and 27 native helpers; that in China of 24 missionaries and 8 native helpers; in Japan of 16 missionaries and 27 native helpers; in Turkey of 4 missionaries and 14 native helpers; in Scandinavia there are 8 missionaries, in England 9, in Africa 2. (In the appendix will be found a list of the names of the missionaries and of their respective fields. Ten new missionaries were

sent out in September, 1898, whose names appear in that list.)

5.   The work of the Foreign Society is increasing year by year, but the men and the means at the disposal of the Executive Committee are not at all equal to the demand for help that comes continually from the fields. Preachers and pastors, evangelists and physicians, teachers and nurses are needed; new stations are calling us and should be answered; church and school buildings, and homes and hospitals are necessities to successful and enduring work; ten men and ten dollars could be used for every one that is at hand.   The society, to use the fine figure of the Corresponding Secretary, "Is like a tree planted by the rivers of water.   Its growth from the first has been constant and vigorous."   Its income each year has broken the record of former ones until last year it reached the sum of $106,222.88.   This was a great joy to our brotherhood and to our missionaries.   And yet what is it among so many!   It came from one-third of our churches, and from less by far than one-third of the people calling themselves distinctively Christians. We must not pause, but pray and work till every church is reached, and every professed follower of Christ has an opportunity to prove

himself Christly in his gifts to the world-wide cause of Christ.

The information given in the following pages is the latest available, and if the statistical part of it should seem disproportionately large, we beg the readers to reflect that it is quite impossible in so few pages to give fullness of literary finish to an adequate statement of so large a work.

QUESTIONS: 1. When was this society organized? 2. Who are its present officers? 3. What officers compose its executive committee, and what are the powers of that committee? 4. What is the object of the society? 5. How many missions has this society? How many stations? 6. How many workers is it supporting? 7. What was the income of the society last year? 8. What per cent. of the churches contribute to the society? What per cent. of the members?

CHAPTER III.

OUR FIELDS AND FORCES IN INDIA.

1. HURDA.—*Statistics:* Membership, 68; scholars enrolled in Sunday-school, 396; enrolled in day school, 144; native evangelists, 3; native helpers and teachers, 10; raised for

all purposes by the church, $85; contributed
by the missionaries, $592.

2.   G. L. Wharton, one of our oldest mis-

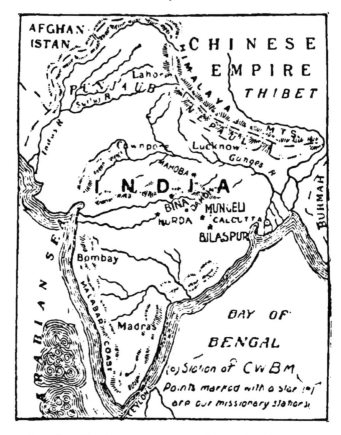

sionaries in India, reports that during the year
1897 he gave himself to preaching, famine relief, and superintending the medical and leper

work. A leper asylum consisting of seven
buildings was begun and finished, not only
providing a home for lepers, but furnishing relief work for many famine sufferers. In addition to this, relief work was carried on in
many villages and out-stations. In one a well
was dug under the direction of a native helper,
to the great joy of the people. In another a
hospital and dwelling for the preacher and
physician were built. Mr. Wharton closes his
report with the following paragraph, which
may be taken as an example of the merciful
and Christly ministries of all our workers in
India:

"The most extensive relief work we have
done has been the free distribution of help.
Grain for food and seed, thread, bamboos,
leather, wood, clothing, etc., have been given,
or the money with which to buy, to many thousands. Widows, orphans, blind, aged, crip-
pled, lepers, and the hungry, helpless, poor
have been supplied, and are being supplied
from our out-stations and from Hurda. More
than sixty villages of helpless farmers and poor
have been visited and helped, and more than a
thousand persons are now being provided for
in our daily ministrations, and with it all we
are preaching the Gospel daily. All help is

given in the name of Jesus. I cannot close
these brief notes without saying that the extensive preaching of the Word and famine relief have been possible only through the generous gifts of Christian friends in many lands,
and the faithful and capable assistance of Ya-
kub Massih, in Hurda; Nathoo Lal, in Charwa; Jagannath, in Rahatgaon, and M. J. Shah
and John Panna in Timarni. We have all
been wonderfully blessed by God with health
and good cheer. God is speaking to India by
severe judgments, famine and plague, pestilence and earthquake, as well as by grace and
mercy, and terribly trying as it is to live in the
midst of famine, to hear the constant unsatis-
fied cry for bread, to see the starving and dying
and dead, yet I take it as a God-sent privilege
and opportunity to make him known among
the heathen.''

3. Mrs. Emma R. Wharton has a self-
sustaining book store for the sale and distribution of Bibles and tracts. She frequently
accompanies her husband on his preaching
tours, assists in caring for the leper asylum
and in hospital work, and with a native helper
spends much time in zenana visitation.

4. Dr. C. C. Drummond has charge of the
medical work. The society has in Hurda a

hospital, two dispensaries and a leper asylum. Samson Powar is a native medical helper. His report may also be taken as an example of the heartiness and efficiency with which many a convert enters upon Christly ministrations to his own countrymen.

He says, "Most of my time is spent at the hospital looking after the in-door and out-door patients, and in distributing the daily supplies to the lepers. For the half year ending June 30th, the statistics are as follows: Out-door patients, 416; in-door patients, 77; lepers, 45. At the hospital I teach the patients every evening. Some commit to memory the Ten Commandments and the Lord's Prayer, and some Bible stories. I teach the lepers twice a week, and my brethren and missionaries also teach them on other days. The condition of the lepers is improving; their ulcers are drying, and they seem much better. Please pray for our work here that many may be led to seek Him who can save to the uttermost."

5. Miss Hattie L. Judson was a beloved and efficient member of the Hurda force. Her report has special pathos and interest, being in itself remarkable, and being her last statement of her earthly work. She says,

"Two months were spent in caring for

Miss Thompson, who was ill. I have taught in my girls' school, in Sunday-school, and three days in the week went to teach a young Christian woman in her own home. From October 10th to January 4th I was in Mahoba helping to nurse Miss Frost, and, when able, assisting in the work at that station. I spent about two months touring among the villages about Hurda. I visited ninety villages altogether and told the good news to 4,300 persons. The majority of these had never heard before of the Savior. From April 3rd to July 1st I was again in Mahoba, where I came in response to an urgent call to help these workers, who are short-handed, owing to illness. Since I have been here one more worker has been sent away for a much-needed rest. I have lent a helping hand to the work these ladies are doing. I have taught in the school, nursed the sick, fed the hungry, and showed these poor little starvelings that I love them by caring for them. Since I have been here 17,602 meals have been given away, and 190 starving boys and girls gathered in. These children have been fed and clothed; their sicknesses treated, and they have been taught about the Savior's love for them. The only difficulties I have encountered this year have been those which always accompany Christian work among people who are opposed to Jesus and the worship of the only true God. The villagers are ready listeners, but their hearts are full of love for a false faith, and the seed of the kingdom is given but little room to grow in. Miss Thompson and I, when at home, make it our practice to have daily Bible lessons with our servants. On Sunday we have a service with poor persons, after which we give them rice and lentils. I have put into the work, of my own funds, $212 this year."

While this report was being read by our brotherhood at Indianapolis the sad news of her death was brought to the convention, and the committee on India introduced the following clause into their report.

"During the Convention tidings of the death of Miss Judson have been received. She fell a martyr to the cause of her Lord—the cause of humanity. In her effort to save a fellow worker from the jaws of death, she yielded up her own life. Heaven is peopled with such choice spirits."

Other workers in the Hurda mission are Mrs. H. L. Jackson, Miss Mary Thompson and G. W. Coffman. Native workers in addition to Samson Powar, who is named above, are M.

J. Shah, John Panna, Nathoo Lal and Jagannath.   Among the out-stations are Timarni,
Charwa, Rahatgaon.

6.   BILASPUR.—*Statistics:*   Membership a
year ago, 35; added since, 12; present strength,
46 ; scholars enrolled in Sunday-school, 125 ; in
day school, 64; native teachers and helpers 3.

Mr. and Mrs. M. D. Adams are the missionaries at this station.   They report that more
room is needed to accommodate the people who
wish to attend the Lord's day services, and
that the number who have asked to be baptized is far in excess of those who are deemed
properly instructed and thoroughly sincere.
Out of a poverty deeper than is ever known
among Americans this little church contributed
last year a total of $77.15; $21.47 for repairs
on their chapel; $39 08 for their cemetery ;
and $16.60 for the famine sufferers.

A paragraph from Mr. Adams' report describing the difficulties of his work fairly repre-
sents the whole field in India, and should be
carefully studied by all who would cultivate a
prayerful sympathy with our missionaries.
He says:

"The difficulties we encounter are many
and great.   Christianity can not gain this
stronghold of darkness without a long and

fierce conflict; it is a conflict from the first to last against an idolatrous faith; against cruel and heathenish customs; against ingrained habits of evil, and against lingering superstition. Even when converts have entered the company of believers, our conflict seems but just begun. Some of the brethren think there is nothing wrong in buying a wife at $3. They say it is an established custom of long standing, and if we do not conform to it how are we to get wives? I tell them that lying and stealing are long-standing evils, and that I know a country where good wives are to be had for less than $3, and that they have only to act righteously, and they will get them for nothing. Some of the brethren also see very little reason why they should so far observe the Lord's day as to refrain from all work and trade. They also find it difficult to overcome all forms of superstition and caste prejudice. They believe the missionary should be accessible night and day for all sorts of petitions and tales of sorrow and suffering. They believe he understands all sorts of diseases, and has vast sources of remedy at hand for every complaint. Others entertain the idea that the church is an alms-giving institution, and the missionary a disburser of charity, with un-

limited supplies for all comforts. There is no
doubt that this is the enemy's most successful
movement against the gospel of Christ, which
teaches that food, and raiment, and homes,
and lands, and silver, and gold, and precious
stones, are all essentially transient and perish-
able, while faith and love and righteousness of
life shall last forever; but as great as are these
obstacles which we encounter, they are not
beyond the strength of the arm of our God.
'We have no might against this great company that cometh against us; neither know
we what to do, but our eyes are upon thee, O
God.'"

8. MUNGELI. — *Statistics :*   Membership
one year ago, 16; added since, 10; present
membership, 26; scholars enrolled in Sunday-
school, 70; in day school, 30; native evangelists, 2; native teachers, 2; medical assistant, 1; women workers, 2; amount raised for
all purposes by church, $3.60; amount contrib-
uted by missionaries, $68.00.

This station is in the hands of E. M. Gordon and Mrs. Dr. Anna Gordon.   In addition
to the church and Sunday School they have an
orphanage and a hospital.   Many hungry children have been cared for, and within one year
Mrs. Gordon reports 5,000 patients treated.

To her patients she tells the story of Jesus daily. She is teaching six women to read and write, and is training one girl as a nurse. All these are preparing for work in the neighboring villages. She has a Sunday afternoon class for women; she teaches them to read the Bible and to offer Christian prayers.

9. DAMOH.—*Statistics:* Membership, 19; pupils in Sunday-school 90; in day schools, 107.

The force in this station consists of John G. McGavran, Mrs. Helen A. McGavran, Dr. Mary T. McGavran, W. E. Rambo, Mrs. Kate Rambo, Miss Josepha Franklin, and Miss Stella Franklin. Their work is quite similar to that of the other stations except that in addition to the orphanage undertaken by the missionaries they were entrusted with the government orphanage during the famine. Many hundreds of children were cared for by them, and Mr. McGavran says:

"Could you see the little armies of woe-begone, gaunt, naked little wretches who come to us from the poor-house and relief works, dying, not so much from the want of food, as from want of proper food and care, and later see the same little heathens smiling, clothed and getting fat under the untiring efforts of the Misses Franklin, you would feel rejoiced at it beyond measure. All told, we have 400 children, whose daily needs have to be looked after from hour to hour."

QUESTIONS: 1. How many members in Hurda, India? 2. How many pupils in the Sunday-schools? 3. How many in the day schools? 5. Describe the work of missionary G. L. Wharton. 5. What asylum is there at Hurda? 6. What other buildings? 7. Describe the work of Mrs. Emma Wharton, of Dr. C. C. Drummond, and of Sampson Powar. 8. Describe the work and death of Miss Hattie L. Judson. 9. How many members in the church in Bilaspur? 10. How many pupils in the Sunday-school? 11. Who are the missionaries at this station? 12. Name some of the hardships and difficulties of their work. 13. How many members in the church in Mungeli? 14. Who are the missionaries there? 15. What charitable institutions have they? 16. What is the church membership in Damoh? 17. How many missionaries are there? 18. Describe their work.

CHAPTER IV.

OUR FIELDS AND FORCES IN CHINA.

1. There are five stations in our China mission. They are Nankin, Shanghai, Wuhu, Chu Cheo, and Lu Cheo Fu. There are four-

teen missionaries, ten of whom are married, and eight native helpers. There are 204 native Christians, 43 pupils in boarding school, 113

The points marked with a star (*) are our mission stations.

in day school, and 165 in Sunday-school. 18,-125 patients were treated in the hospitals, from whom was received $910.82.

2. NANKIN.—This was the city chosen by Dr. W. E. Macklin in 1886 for the beginning of our work in China. A description of Nankin as a typical Chinese city will give much food for reflection to the thoughtful student. In his "Circuit of the Globe" the Secretary of our Foreign Society, A. McLean, describes it in a few graphic sentences. He and his friends had to go out sight seeing on donkeys. "No carriage could make its way through such narrow and crowded streets. The viceroy has built a wide road from one end of the city to the other, on which horses and carriages may be seen, but on no other. A boy goes with each donkey to twist his tail to make him go, and to make the appropriate remarks when things go wrong, and to clear the way when it is blocked. The sights and smells soon convince one that he is in a heathen city. Though there are half a million souls within the walls of Nankin there are no sewers and no sanitary provisions whatever. Large ponds are covered with green scum. Gutters are filled with garbage and filth. Coffins and graves are everywhere in sight. Houses are plastered with charms to keep away evil spirits and disease. In times of pestilence the streets are lined with idols and altars. Cleanliness would do more

to prevent the plagues than all the prayers and offerings.''

3. Here Dr. Macklin has a hospital well equipped and two dispensaries. He is assisted by his sister, Dr. Daisy Macklin. Theirs is a most beneficent work. (See Chapter X.) They preach to all their patients, and last year there were over twenty baptisms, mainly the work, says Dr. Macklin, of a poor tramp baptized the year before.

4. In this city Prof. F. E. Meigs has a school for boys, which is attended by as many as he can take. He teaches the Bible every day, has an Endeavor Society and Sunday-school, and last year had the joy of baptizing eight of his pupils. He has a printing department furnished with a small press on which are printed small tracts and books in Chinese. Last year fourteen boys were learning the trade.

Miss Emma Lyon is connected with the work in Nankin. She has erected a school building in which she conducts a day school for girls. She has also near the gate-house a school for boys and girls, and has organized an Endeavor Society.

Other missionaries in Nankin are Frank Garrett and Mrs. Ethel Garrett, Mrs. Dorothy DeLaney Macklin, and Miss Mary Kelly.

In addition to the work in Nankin, our missionaries go out on preaching tours many miles in extent; they are often gone for days at a time, and they preach in scores of towns and villages.

5.   Mr. E. T. Williams must also be named as among our earliest and most efficient missionaries in China. Though not at present employed by our Foreign Society, he is very active in the work, preaching constantly at various places, and editing the *Missionary Review*, a distinctively religious monthly, which goes to all the missionaries in China.

The church in Nankin has 84 members, 45 of whom were added last year. The boarding school for boys has 38 pupils, the day school 14, and the Sunday-school 60.

6.   SHANGHAI.—*Statistics:* Membership one year ago, 43; added since, 12; net gain, 8; present membership, 51; scholars enrolled in Sunday-school, 61; native evangelists, 4; native teachers and helpers, 3; amount raised for all purposes by the church, $33.25; amount contributed by the missionaries, $356.25.

This is one of the most important cities in all the east. It is the New York of China, and its influence is growing year by year. It is a great literary center, and its volume of business surpasses that of the national capital, Pekin. James Ware is pastor of the Central Church; he teaches, preaches, evangelizes, superintends the school, examines the pupils weekly, has charge of four out-stations, one of which is a walled city of a million inhabitants, and is general secretary of the Endeavor work in China.

Mrs. Lillie Ware has a girl's school with above twenty pupils. She devotes much time to work among women, and has a faithful helper in Mrs. Li, an efficient Bible woman.

7. Mr. and Mrs. W. P. Bentley are also located at Shanghai. Mr. Bentley has work in the two stations, Tsa-Sao and Yang-King. He has a day school in Shanghai, and is erecting a building that will combine a chapel, Sunday-school room, and class rooms. He is teaching the Christians self-support, and training them to take care of their own sick.

8. LU CHEO FU.—This city of 75,000 inhabitants is the ancestral home of Li Hung Chang, the Viceroy of China. A million people are easily accessible beyond its walls. Dr. James Butchart and Mr. and Mrs. C. B. Titus have recently selected it as their field of labor, and to them it is virgin soil, for they are the only Protestant missionaries there.

9. CHU CHEO.—The work in this place is

closely connected with that in Yu Ho Tsz, and since the recent sad death of A. F. H. Saw it is in the hands of Mrs. Saw and Mr. and Mrs. W. R. Hunt. This station has been especially unfortunate in losing its workers, E. P. Herndon having been called away in 1897. Of the death of Mr. Saw Dr. Macklin writes:

" Bro. Saw is dead. He died yesterday of the pestilence—typhus fever. There is a famine in the country north of Nankin, and about one thousand died of starvation around and in Nankin in a few days during the early springtime. For months he labored with the poor famine sufferers, trying to provide shelter and clothing from the cold and storm, food for the hungry, and medical relief for the sick and diseased. How could one poor man struggle with such a vast need? He could not relieve a tithe of the suffering, and his sympathetic heart nearly broke. Overwork and the depressing hopelessness of this attempted relief work told on his physical condition, and his good wife took him to Shanghai for a rest, but he had doubtless the germs of the pestilence contracted while trying to serve the poor. Typhus makes quick work with the nervously depressed, and so we have lost a good man. The Chinese all loved Bro. Saw. The official and scholar loved

him for his loving heart.   The poor, and even
the beggar loved him, for he knew no caste,
but loved all.   I have traveled most of the
country over which Bro. Saw worked, and
everybody speaks well of him.   His influence
will tell for good for many years.''

10.   WUHU.—*Statistics:* Membership one
year ago, 23; added since, 5; present membership, 28; scholars in Sunday-school, 16; day
school, 16; native evangelists, 1; native teacher and helper, 1; amount raised by the
church, $15.

Mr. and Mrs. Charles E. Molland and Mr.
and Mrs. T. J. Arnold are in charge of this
station.   They report that crowds come to
the daily preaching of the Gospel, and that
thousands have been hearers of it.   The ruling
classes have exchanged courtesies with them
and have given them a standing in the eyes of
the people.   There is great need of medical
work in Wuhu.

QUESTIONS: 1. How many stations are there in
China? 2. How many missionaries? 3. How many
native Christians? 4. How many patients were treated
in the hopitals last year? 5. When and in what city
did the work in China begin? 6. Describe Nankin
as typical of heathen cities? 7. What physicians are
in charge of the medical work in Nankin? 8. What

schools have we in Nankin, and by whom are they conducted? 9. What other work is done by the missionaries? 10. What periodical is published and by whom? 11. Why is Shanghai an important city? 12. What is the church membership there? 13. Who is pastor of the church? 14. Describe his work. 15. What help has Mrs. Ware? 16. What other missionaries are in Shanghai? 17. What is the population of Lu Cheo Fu? 18. What is its importance as a center? 19. What able missionary died at Chu Cheo? 20. How many members in the church at Wuhu? 21. What encouragements have the missionaries there?

CHAPTER V.

OUR FIELDS AND FORCES IN JAPAN.

1. *Total Statistics:* Membership one year ago, 335; added since, 36; lost by death, 2; present membership, 369; scholars enrolled in the Sunday-schools, 921; scholars enrolled in day schools, 243; in the English night school, 40; students in college, 7; native evangelists employed, 8; teachers and helpers, 19; amount raised for all purposes by the church, $160.05; amount contributed by the missionaries, $1,339.71. If all the moneys given by the missionaries were included, the total would be much larger than this.

2.   TOKYO.—This city is the capital of the
nation.   It is a city of above a million and a
half of people.   In it are located ten of our

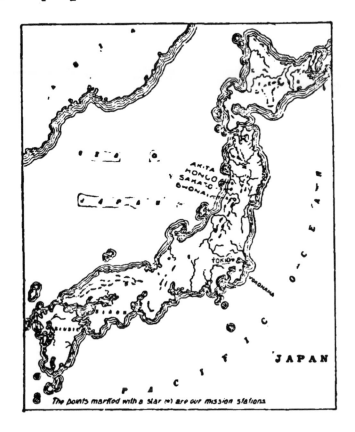

The points marked with a star (*) are our mission stations.

workers.   Mr. and Mrs. C. E. Garst are in
Tsukiji;   Miss Kate V. Johnson is in Hongo ;
Mr. and Mrs. Frank Marshall and Mr. and

Mrs. H. H. Guy are in Koishikawa; Miss Lavinia Oldham and Miss Mary Rioch are in
Ushigome. Miss Loduska Wirick is also in
Tokio. In the city there are three organized
churches with a total membership of 152; there
are 12 meeting places, 9 Sunday-schools with
an attendance of 594, and 6 day schools with
an attendance of 243.

3. In addition to daily preaching at a
street chapel in Honjo Ku, near Akita, Mr.
Garst preaches regularly on Sunday and Tues-
day nights. On one of the principal streets in
Ushigome Ku he has an industrial bakery
which besides paying expenses supports one
student.

4. H. H. Guy has a men's Bible school
with 7 students in attendance. He teaches
five hours a day, and assists the native pastor,
Mr. Nishioka, in his work in the Koishikawa
church.

Mrs. H. H. Guy has a school for poor children, and holds frequent meetings weekly for
women and children, and distributes much
Christian literature.

5. Miss Loduska Wirick with the assistance of a native woman has a mission in Ushigome, and a large class of girls studying the
Bible. She says, "I carry on evangelistic

work among the people and am much encouraged by the prospects.''

6. Miss Kate V. Johnson says, '' For another year's labor in Hongo we thank God an I take courage. The foundations have been strengthened, and good seed has been sown. That none have been baptized does not indicate a falling off in interest. There is much to encourage us for characters are being formed and principles of self support grow stronger day by day.''

Miss Lavinia Oldham and Miss Mary Rioch are associated in work in Ushigome. They have a Charity School, two Sunday-schools, a home for girls, and a Bible Woman's Training School. During the last year they have built a church.

AKITA.—The church in Akita enjoys the distinction of being our first church in Japan. It was organized by George T. Smith, our first missionary to Japan. In point of numbers it is yet the strongest church in the empire, having three preaching places with 72 members, and three Sunday-schools with 80 scholars and teachers. Noto San is the native evangelist and has large audiences. Here is the memorial chapel to Josephine W. Smith, the former wife of George T. Smith, a saintly woman who gave her life to the work, and of whom it has been well said, "Her purity and devotion are the best imitation of Christ."

JOSEPHINE W. SMITH MEMORIAL CHAPEL,
AKITA, JAPAN.

The chapel was erected entirely by the gifts of the children known as the Junior Builders.

E. S Stevens and his wife, Dr. Nina A. Stevens, are in charge of the work in Akita. Mr. Stevens says, "It is a common opinion among experienced missionaries that Japan is now the hardest field in the world. The entire school system is opposed to Christianity. The Governor of one province dismissed one teacher for no other reason than that he was a Christian." Mr. Stevens is constantly engaged in teaching Bible classes and evening class s in English, and in preparing native disciples for teaching and preaching, and in conversing with numerous inquirers.

Dr. Nina A. Stevens, in addition to caring for three Bible classes, a Christian Aid Society, a women's meeting for unbelievers, two Sunday-schools, and a sewing class, sees hundreds of patients and distributed in one year 7,510 pages of literature. (See Chapter X)

9. SHIZUOKA AND FUKUSHIMA.—These stations have been opened but a short time. The former is in charge of Mr. and Mrs. R. L. Pruett, and the latter of Mr. and Mrs. M. B. Madden.

A number of native evangelists have been employed in the Japan mission and are doing good work. Y. Kudo at Innai may be taken as an example of the more efficient ones among them. He preaches to audiences ranging from 75 to 100; and has many inquirers. Last year he baptized 7 believers.

QUESTIONS: 1. How many native Christians in our mission in Japan? 2. How many Sunday-school scholars? 3. How many in day schools? 4. How many native evangelists are employed? 5. What is the capital of Japan, and what is its population? 7. How many of our missionaries are located in this city? 7. How many churches and members? 8. How often does Mr. Garst preach, and what industrial work does he superintend? 9. Describe the work of Mr. and Mrs. H. H. Guy, Miss Wirick, Miss Johnson, and Miss Oldham, and Miss Rioch. 10. Where was our first mission in Japan? 11. What noted chapel is there, and by whose gifts was it erected? 12. Who have charge of the work in Akita? 13. Describe the work of Dr. Nina A. Stevens. 14. What stations have been recently opened in Japan?

CHAPTER VI.

OUR FIELDS AND FORCES IN TURKEY.

1. This is a field to excite our utmost sympathy and call forth our prayers. In no part of the world has the work of our missionaries during the last three years been so hazardous, and the confession of Christ fraught with so much persecution. The cruelties and indignities of the Turkish soldiers are too fearful for description. They have gouged out

the eyes of men and strung them like beads on
a string; they have inflicted on Christian
wómen nameless indignities; and while recit-

ing verses of the Koran they have cut the
throats of hundreds of young men.   Our faithful missionaries, under such protection as the
American flag afforded them, have stayed by

their work, and are praying for a brighter day.

2. CONSTANTINOPLE, BARDIZAG, SEVAS, ZARAH, GIL DAGOH, ANTIOCH AND BIRIDJEK.—*Statistics:* Number reported last year, 387; added since, 21; net gain, 20; scholars in Sunday-school in Constantinople, 92; native helpers, 8; contributed for missions, $25.50.

Mr. and Mrs. G. N. Shishmanian are located at Constantinople, and have charge of the work there and in the above named stations. The following statements are selected from Mr. Shishmanian's eighteenth annual report. Had he been permitted to engage in visitation this would have been his best report, for the fiery trials of the Christians have kindled a lively interest in their hearts for the word of God. In the face of all opposition there were twenty additions as shown by the report, and the school building has been renewed and enlarged to accommodate 200 pupils. He says, "I congratulate myself on the success of the work at such a time as this when the Turkish government never permits the building or repairing of any Christian church or school in this country. Surely the hand of God is upon us for good."

3. MARSIVAN, HAJI KENI, CAPOU KARA, CHECHARSHAMBEH.—*Statistics:* Number re-

ported last year, 258; added since 2; net gain, 2; scholars enrolled in Sunday-school, 210; average attendance, 184; native helpers, 6; contributed for self-support, $13; amount given by the missionaries, $95.

3. Dr. Garabed Kevorkian has charge of the work at Marsivan and the stations above named. In Marsivan and Capou Kara he has four schools, which, together with the churches, are doing well in spite of the hardships recently endured. He has preached in Tokat with great acceptance, and prays our Foreign Society to send further help to the field in Turkey. (See Chapter X.)

4. In the ancient New Testament city of Smyrna we have a little church, the present condition of which is too sadly like that of the ancient one, of which it is said, Rev. ii: 9, "I know thy works, thy tribulation, and thy poverty, but thou art rich." John Johnson has recently taken charge of the work. He is seeking to gather together the scattered church of thirty or forty members, and hopes to do some work among the Moslems.

5. A. L. Chapman, for several years the pastor of the church in Mt. Healthy, Ohio, and recently a student in the University of Chicago, has been appointed by the Executive

Committee of our Foreign Society to the work in Turkey. We should not cease to pray that he and all his co-workers, not forgetting the fourteen native helpers, may be kept and abundantly blessed in that dreadful field.

QUESTIONS: 1. Describe Turkish warfare. 2. Who are the missionaries at Constantinople? 3. How many members in that station and its out-stations? 4. How many children in the Constantinople Sunday-school? 5. What is the attitude of the Turkish Government toward the work? 6. Describe the work of Dr. Garabed Kevorkian. 7. In what city named in the New Testament have we a church? 8. Who has recently been appointed to the work in Turkey?

CHAPTER VII.

OUR FIELDS AND FORCES IN SCANDINAVIA.

1. The work in this country was begun by Dr. A. Holck in 1876. This able missionary and man of God was born and educated in Jutland, and came to this country to engage in the practice of medicine. He had a lucrative practice in the city of Cincinnati when he united with the Central Christian Church, and

was asked to return to his own people as a preacher of the primitive Gospel. As a dissenter from the teachings of the state church he knew he would encounter much opposition, but he gave up his practice and undertook the work upon which God has seen fit to look graciously, as shown by the statistics given below.

2. The state church is distinctively Lutheran, and following the usual course of state churches it has grown cold in its formalism and deadly in its sacramentalism. It is of course correspondingly intolerant. "The people believe they are regenerated in baptism and kept saved by the sacraments. Dr. Holck was taken before the courts for baptizing a minor. Some rough fellows threatened to throw him out of the window. The court, however, decided in his favor." Infant baptism is the universal practice and re-baptism is thought to be the sin against the Holy Spirit. There are but two classes of infants, those who are baptized or Christened, and those who are heathen, and who if they die are damned. Dr. Holck's mother said to him: "If you had a child I would steal it and have it Christened. I could not sleep till this was done."

3. There is a great field in Scandinavia

for the presentation of Christ as he presents himself in the New Testament. Dr. Holck thinks that with ten thousand dollars a year he could take the whole of that country. With ample men and means at hand there is no reason why the land of Gustavus Adolphus, the defender of Protestantism in the sixteenth century, should not become the home of undenominational Christianity, and therefore also an evangelizing force in all the earth.

4.   DENMARK.—In Copenhagen there is a church and mission. The church building is the best in the city belonging to dissenters, and cost $22,000.00. There are 186 members; the Sunday-school has 10 teachers and 75 pupils.

5.   NORWAY.—In this country there are twenty churches and five brethren who give themselves to the ministry. Ten of the churches have modest houses of worship. There are in all 960 members, and 250 pupils enrolled in the Sunday-schools.

In Sweden the work has but just begun. There is a young church of 12 members, and a Sunday-school of 15 pupils.

QUESTIONS: 1. Who began the work in Scandinavia? 2. What was he with reference to the State

Church? 3. What sacrifice did he make in order to preach to his own people? 4. What is the spiritual condition of the State Church? 5. What is the belief of the people with regard to baptism? 6. How are infants classified? 7. What does Dr. Holck think of the outlook in Scandinavia? 8. Describe the work in Denmark. In Norway. In Sweden.

CHAPTER VIII.

OUR FIELDS AND FORCES IN ENGLAND.

1. Upon first thought it seems incongruous that we should send missionaries to England, remembering that she is reckoned as among the most Christian nations in the world. She is our mother country, she was evangelized many centuries before America was discovered, and she gives more for the evangelization of heathen peoples to-day than all other countries combined.

Our reasons for the English mission are in the first place, the simple fact that when our Foreign Society began its work the way seemed providentially opened toward England. There were no missionaries available for other lands, and many English brethren, among whom was Timothy Coop, a generous and saintly man, were pleading earnestly for help. Many of our American Christians felt the force of their plea, and the work was accordingly undertaken.

Another, and perhaps the chief reason must be sought in the religious conditions of England, for which the student is referred to Chapter XVII.

2. The following tabulated statement shows quite accurately the condition of the work at the present time:

CHURCHES.	PASTORS.	Number Members Last Year.	Increase.	Decrease.	Number Members This Year.
Hornsey Tabernacle..........	W. Durbau....	81	10	...	91
Tasso Tabernacle, London...	H. A. McKenzie	66	....	16	50
West London Tabernacle....	....	450	....	46	404
Southampton	H. L. Gow......	141	8	....	149
Birkenhead	E. Brearley	233	5	....	238
Chester................	E. M. Todd.....	292	15	....	307
Saltney.....................	....	39	11	....	50
Liverpool	J. H. Bicknell...	148	....	4	144
Southport...............	A. Johnson.....	120	11	11	120
Cheltenham..................	T. H. Bates.....	76	15	....	91
Gloucester..................	E. H. Spring....	200	23	....	223
Lancaster..................	J. H. Versey....	19	7	....	26
Ingleton.	do. once per Mo.	15	....	...	15
Margate....................	Geo. Rapkin..	25	3	....	28
14 churches.	11 pastors.	51,90	108	77	1,936

3. These churches have property valued at $137,080.00. They raised last year for all purposes $17,463.11, of which $1,077.95 was for missions; the rest for self-support. They have a regular attendance at their Sunday-schools of about 2,000. It may be noted that their net increase last year in membership was only 31. Recently however there have been gratifying additions to several churches. The June number of the *Missionary Intelligencer* reports the following baptisms: In Birkenhead, 3; Chester, 5; Gloucester, 51; Hornsey, 8; Margate, 2; Southampton, 36; Tasso, 7; other additions make the number for the month 122.

4. To cause England and America to see the Christ as he presents himself in the Gospels is ultimately to bring to the whole world a purer teaching, since God is using these two nations as his foremost evangelizing agencies. Already from England and Canada there have gone out a number of our most efficient missionaries to the foreign fields.

QUESTIONS: 1. Why are we doing missionary work in England? 2. How many pastors are at work there? 3. How many members in the churches? 4. What is the valuation of Church property? 5. What is the attendance in Sunday-schools? 6. What feature of the work has given recent satisfaction? 7. What if England and America could be united in preaching the Gospel in its purity? 8. What saintly Englishman has greatly helped the work?

CHAPTER IX.

OUR FIELDS AND FORCES IN AFRICA.

1. This great continent has been the riddle of the centuries. Africa has no better emblem than the Egyptian sphinx, massive and mysterious. But of late she is yielding to the consecration and heroism of missionaries, the diplomacy of statesmen, and the enterprise of traders and capitalists. David Livingstone crossed and re-crossed South Africa, and penetrated Central Africa, saying that "the end of geographical exploration would be the beginning of Christian evangelization," and praying that God would heal the open sore of the terrible slave trade. Henry M. Stanley, inspired by Livingstone's zeal, crossed the continent from east to west, occupying 999 days, and discovering the sources of the Nile and the Congo, and tracing the latter river through more than two thousand miles of its course.

Livingstone drew the eyes of the civilized world to Africa, and Stanley paved the way for the opening of her immense interior.

2. Africa has 12,000,000 square miles. Her area is equal to that of North America and Europe combined, or more than 4 times that of the United States. Her population is at least 200,000,000, or nearly three times that of the United States.

3. The basin of the Congo is the largest in the world except that of the Amazon. This one river drains a territory equal to the sum total of all the lands that pour their waters out through the Danube, the Euphrates, the Nile

and the Volga. We have yet to realize the immensity of this region, and our best comparison is our own Mississippi, the basin of which is estimated at 1,250,000 square miles, while that of the Congo is 1,639,000.

4. The Congo itself is between three and four thousand miles long. Two at least of its tributaries are magnificent rivers, the Mobangi on the north and the Kasai on the south. Besides these there are numerous tributaries and tributaries of tributaries, until the total shore line of the great system reaches the astonishing figure of 22,000 miles—more than that of all Europe including the British Isles. It has been shown that if Europe could have substituted for all her rivers this one river system she would need no other.

5. For centuries this vast water-way was hidden from the civilized world by the rapids below Stanley Pool. Its discovery by Stanley was like that of a new continent. Ninety miles inward from its mouth the Congo is navigable. The next 250 miles of its course is rendered impassable by reason of 32 cataracts. Then again for thousands of miles the river is an open highway. Until recently it was a 25-days' journey past these cataracts, and goods had to be transported on the heads of

black men.   Mules were worthless; they could not stand the climate and the labor.   Within the last few months a railroad has been opened from Matadi below the rapids to Leopoldville above them, and now the trip is made in one day with comfort and safety.   This railway opens to the outer world a population estimated at 40,000,000, and a wealth of natural resources surpassing that of the Mississippi valley when it was discovered three centuries ago.   This wealth is destined for use, and these millions of human beings will have a history.   It remains for Christians to say by their prayers, their gifts, and their missionary pastors and teachers what that history shall be.

6.   At the instance of King Leopold II, of Belgium, a conference of the nations of Christendom was called in Berlin, Nov. 15th, 1884. It continued in session till February, 1885. Accredited delegates were present from fourteen nations, including Germany, France, Russia, Turkey, Great Britain, and the United States.   At the cost of five years of arduous and dangerous labor in which he well nigh lost his life, Henry M. Stanley was enabled to lay before this conference treaties signed by 450 kings or native chieftains in the Congo Basin. By mutual agreement upon the basis of these

treaties the Congo Free State was created, covering a territory of 1,508,000 square miles, with a population of 39,000,000. Over these vast peoples and regions it was decreed that there should be, "Liberty of conscience and religious toleration; the free and public exercise of every creed, the right to erect religious buildings, and to organize missions belonging to every creed without any restriction or impediment whatever." This is the most notable example of the creation out of barbarism of a free state under the guidance and protection of civilized and Christianized nations in the world's history. "It was the triumph of Christian principle over human selfishness. Europe for once agreed to do what was right by the helpless, and to prevent others from doing what was wrong." The one mournful mistake of the conference was the failure to prohibit the importation of rum into this region. Slavery is prohibited, and commerce, science, and Christianization are protected and promoted.

7. Looking at all this we cannot fail to recognize the hand of God in the working of a double wonder, first that so many civilized nations should unite in the protection and development of so great and helpless a region, and

secondly that so many uncivilized tribes should unite in accepting such help and protection.

Since the establishment of the Congo Free State immigration is pouring in; capital is seeking investment there; mines are being opened; wealth is being developed, and gold-seekers are abundant.

Our Lord's hosts seeking souls should keep pace with the hosts of mammon. From the north and east Roman Catholics and Mohammedans are pouring into this region. Bishop Hartzell says: "The day of the black races has dawned, and Africa is to be the chief scene of their redemption. On this continent are crystallizing the forces for tremendous conflicts, commercial, racial and spiritual."

A number of societies have entered this part of Africa, but as yet only a beginning has been made. Two years ago it was reported that there were but 1,500 native Christians in all this vast region.

8. A notable and hopeful characteristic of the African is his teachableness. Spite of his sin and degradation, his cruelty and human sacrifices, his fetishism and cannibalism, his tribal wars and the horrible cruelties of the slave hunters, the Negro readily acquires faith in his white teacher, and his childlike soul is

accessible to the calls of Christ. A missionary
of Uganda said to Mr. John R. Mott: "Five
years ago we had 400 baptisms; four years ago,
800; three years ago, 1,600; two years ago,
3,400; the past year, nearly 7,000."

This chapter is made to deal chiefly with
the Congo region because our Foreign Society
is locating a mission there. In 1897 Dr. H.
N. Biddle and E. E. Farris were sent to the
Upper Congo, with instructions to seek an
available and promising field for work.

QUESTIONS: 1. Name two of the greatest ex-
plorers of Africa. 2. How large is Africa as compared
with the United States? 3. What is her population?
4. Describe the Congo River. 5. Why was the Congo
basin so long undiscovered? 6. How is it now
reached? 7. What is its population? 8. When and
at whose instance was the Congo Free State established? 9. What are its decrees with respect to religious toleration? 10. What classes are pouring
into the Congo region? 11. Who are our missionaries there?

CHAPTER X.

OUR MEDICAL MISSIONS.

The Foreign Society is carrying on medical work at four stations in India, three in

China, one in Japan, and one in Turkey.

The stations in India are at Hurda, Timarni, Mungeli, and Damoh. Those in China are at Nankin, Chu Cheo, and Lu Cheo Fu. The one in Japan is at Akita.

At Hurda, Timarni, and Mungeli, there are well-equipped hospitals and dispensaries; at Damoh an out-building is used by Dr. McGavran as a substitute for a hospital. The hospital in Hurda stands upon land that was given by a Hindu in token of his appreciation of Dr. C. S. Durand, who began the work in that place. The work is now in charge of Dr. C. C. Drummond, and about 15,000 prescriptions are given out each year. At Timarni, which is an out-station of Hurda, Dr. John Panna, who has charge of the work, treated 2,000 patients during the first year after the hospital was opened. At Mungeli Dr. Anna Gordon has charge. She took her degree in Berlin, and previous to her marriage to E M. Gordon she received $2,000 a year in the capacity of court physician to the Gaekwar of Baroda. During her first year at Mungeli she treated 5,000 patients. Dr. Mary T. McGavran at Damoh has under her care 400 children in the orphanage besides the thousands of afflicted people who apply to her for relief.

She is supported by our sisterhood in England, but is reckoned as a missionary of the Foreign Society.

Nearly all the workers in India give out more or less medicine. Many difficulties are encountered in treating the people of that land. Some refuse to take water and liquid medicine from the hand of the physician lest they should be polluted and lose caste. Women refuse to have male physicians and must for the most part be treated by women. A very interesting feature of the medical work in India is the study that Dr. C. S. Durand has made of leprosy, and his success in the treatment of it, many of his patients being cured, he hopes permanently. Near Hurda he has a leper asylum consisting of seven buildings. The beneficence of this work becomes the more impressive when one reflects that there are a half million of lepers in India, roaming about from place to place as they did in Palestine in the time of the Savior.

In Nankin, China, Dr. W. E. Macklin sees about 16,000 patients each year. In this great work he is assisted by his sister, Dr. Daisy Macklin.

In Chu Cheo W. R. Hunt treats above 2,000 a year. He is not a physician, but has taken some studies under Dr. Macklin, and treats successfully many of the simpler cases of disease, sending the more difficult ones to the hospital in Nankin. He is known far and near as "the doctor," and many times when on preaching tours the Chinese, who otherwise would have killed him, have spared his life because of this.

In Lu Cheo Fu Dr. James Butchart has charge of the work, which has but just begun. Quite recently he performed a surgical operation by which he saved a man's life, and the people were so impressed that they presented him with a memorial tablet bearing the following inscription: "The benevolence done spreads its influence into the whole Middle Kingdom." They came beating drums, and blowing horns, and in ceremonial robes, to hang up this tablet, and that notwithstanding the fact that when the Doctor entered the city a short time before they wanted to drive him out. The same revolution in sentiment has taken place in Nankin, where now the hospital buildings are covered with such scrolls, where the leading business men made a feast when the hospital was opened, and where they frequently subscribe money for its support.

All the missionaries in China go out on

preaching tours carrying supplies of medicine
with them. One is a benefactor in China if
he can but give quinine to ague sufferers, or
extract decayed and aching teeth. Most of
the hospital cases are people who have been
given up by their native doctors. They come
suffering with all sorts of diseases, breaks,
and bruises, and in multitudes of cases Christian science triumphs where superstition and
magic had already failed. The following is
a Chinese receipt for ulcer, "Pulverized ser-
pents, one ounce; wasps and their nests, half
an ounce; centipedes, three ounces; scorpions,
six, and toads, ten ounces; grind thoroughly,
mix with honey, and make into pills."

At Akita, Japan, Dr. Nina A. Stephens
sees about 2,000 patients a year besides giving
instruction to women and children regarding
their health, and training two medical students. Akita is in the northern part of Japan
where the need of medical work is much
greater than in the southern cities, there being
in the latter many well-trained native physicians.

Our one medical missionary in Turkey is
Dr. Garabed Kevorkian. Through the terrible Armenian massacres he was unmolested
because under the blessing of God he had

been able to save the wife of the governor of the province. This ruler said to him, "You are a good man; go on with your work; you shall not be molested." This promise was faithfully kept.

In addition to the above Dr. H. N. Biddle has been sent to the Congo Valley in Africa as an associate of E. E. Faris. He has treated many sick people, and by so doing he has won favor for himself and his associate with both natives and foreigners.

The medical work is secondary to the evangelistic. The cures of the physician open hearts and homes that otherwise would be closed to the truth. All our physicians are preachers and teachers, and all their patients hear the truth, and carry it to their own homes, many of them rejoicing in Jesus Christ as Lord and Savior.

(For the substance of this chapter the author is indebted to A. McLean, the Secretary of our Foreign Society. For the medical work of the C. W. B. M. see Chapter XI.)

QUESTIONS: 1. How many stations in India have medical departments? 2. How many in China? In Japan? In Turkey? 3. How many hospitals in India? 4. Describe the work in Bilaspur. In Timarni. In Mungeli. 5. In what special work is Dr. Durand engaged? 6. Describe the work in Nankin. In Chu Cheo. In Lu Cheo Fu. 7. Why is Japan in less need of medical missions than China, India, and Africa? 8. Describe the work at Akita. 9. Who is our medical missionary in Turkey? 10. Who in Africa? 11. How does the medical work stand related to the evangelistic.

CHAPTER XI.

CHRISTIAN WOMAN'S BOARD OF MISSIONS.

President.....................Mrs. O. A. Burgess.
Corresponding Secretary..Miss Lois A. White.
Treasurer.................. .Miss Mary J. Judson.
Superintendent of Young
   People's Department.....Miss Mattie Pounds.
Place of business, 306 North Delaware St., Indianapolis, Ind.

1. The organization of this society was an answer to prayer. Mrs. Caroline N. Pearre, in answer to inquiries, has given the following account of it: "On the 10th of April, 1874, about 10 o'clock in the morning, at the close of my private devotions, the thought came to me. I promptly conferred with Bro. Munnell, who was then Corresponding Secretary of the General Christian Missionary Convention, to know if he thought it practicable. He responded at once: 'This is a flame of the Lord's kindling, and no man can extinguish it.'"

Correspondence on the part of Mrs. Pearre developed the fact that the hearts of many Godly women were moving in the same direction. Isaac Errett, at that time editor of the *Christian Standard*, and J. H. Garrison, editor at that time and still editor of the *Christian Evangelist*, united in giving to the movement the hearty approval and support of their editorial columns. It is interesting to note that before the organization of the national Board, local societies were formed in various places intended to be auxiliary to such a Board. In response to a call for a convention about seventy-five sisters met in Cincinnati in October, 1874. On the 22nd of that month the Christian Woman's Board of Missions was organized, a constitution adopted, and the place of business fixed at Indianapolis. The motto of the society is, "The love of Christ constraineth us."

2. The objects of the society are, according to Article II of the Constitution, "to maintain preachers and teachers for religious instruction, to encourage and cultivate a missionary spirit and missionary efforts in the churches, to disseminate missionary intelligence, and to secure systematic contributions for such purposes; also to establish and maintain schools and institutions for the education of both males and females."

3. The Constitution also provides for local societies in the churches, acting as auxiliaries

to this Board, and contributing to it the funds derived from the regular monthly offerings of their members. This is usually ten cents per member, and no more systematic and effective plan of giving has been introduced to the churches. The almost constant growth in the receipts of the society is indicative both of the wisdom of the financial plan adopted and of the consecration of our missionary sisterhood. In the year of its organization the income of the society was but $430.00. Ten years later, in 1884, it was $14,418.55. In 1894 it was $59,277.08. Last year it was $62,600.81. In only three years has there been a falling off from the receipts of previous years, and there is every reason to expect continually enlarging receipts in coming years. This is the more emphatically true inasmuch as the society combines the devotional with the practical side of the work, and systematic giving is made to go hand in hand with fervent prayer. The adopted hour for prayer is from 5 to 6 every Lord's day.

4. The Jamaica mission was the first undertaken by this Board. The work in that "land of rare fertility and surpassing beauty" has suffered in several ways, chiefly from the too frequent changes in the force of workers. Spite of all hindrances, however, there are

now 19 churches with a total membership of 1,664, and 9 Endeavor Societies with 286 members. The contributions of these Christians for all purposes in 1877 amounted to $2,755.00.

Jamaica is one of the most beautiful and romantic of the islands of the British West Indies. It is about one-twelfth the size of Illinois, with a population about twice as dense, while its rural population as compared with that of Illinois is about eight times as dense. There are on the island 700,000 people, one in fifty of whom are white; the others are negroes and mulattoes. The mountaineers are described as a vigorous and industrious people, cheery and finely disposed. In the cities many carry in their faces the signs of dissipation and sin.

In addition to the sending of missionaries to the island it is now the policy of the Woman's Board to bring suitable and available young men from Jamaica to the Southern Christian Institute, (See Chapter XIII,) to be educated, with a view to work thereafter in their native land.

(For a list of the stations and workers in Jamaica, the student is referred to the appendix at the close of the book. Similar reference should be made regarding the other fields of the C. W. B. M.)

6. INDIA.—The stations of the Christian
Woman's Board of Missions in India are Bilaspur and Bina, Central Provinces; Deoghur
in Bengal, and Mahoba in the Northwest Provinces.

In 1881 the Foreign Society and the Woman's Board co-operated in opening the work
in India.   Hurda was first entered, and is still
a prosperous station of the Foreign Society.
Later in connection with the missionaries of
the Foreign Board the ladies sent out by the
C. W. B. M., namely Miss Ada Boyd, Miss
Mary Graybiel, and Miss Mary Kingsbury,
moved two hundred miles further inland to
Bilaspur, where there is now a goodly work
permanently established.   The workers are
made comfortable by having for their home a
bungalow, and are equipped for work with a
school house and orphanage, a dormitory and
hospital.   At the orphanage Miss Kingsbury
and her assistants have generally the care of
50 or 60 motherless children.   Miss Boyd, de-
voting herself to zenana work, visits 26 bunga-
lows regularly, some of which are Mohamme-
dan, and some Hindu.   In addition to these
she often visits other homes.   In 1888 the
medical department of the work was opened in
Bilaspur, and is now in charge of Dr. E. C. L.

Miller and his wife, Dr. Lillian B. Miller.

7. At Bina a church has been established with 26 members, 14 of whom were baptized last year. There are two schools; one for boys and one for girls, and zenana work is kept up during a part of each year. The station is in charge of Ben. N. Mitchell, Mrs. Laura V. Mitchell, and Miss Ida Kinsey.

8. At Deoghur, 200 miles west from Calcutta, is the station that was opened by Jane Wakefield Adam, a devout Scotch woman, who went out independent of any church or board, simply praying to be led to the darkest part of India. She was a Baptist, reading her Bible, and praying for Christian union. In 1893 she visited our workers in Bilaspur, and the next year came into the employ of the C. W. B. M., bringing her work with her. Miss M. Alice Spradlin and Miss Bessie Farrar have been sent to her assistance. "These women are lovingly known by the young people of our Mission Bands and Junior Endeavor Societies as Aunt Jane and Cousins Bessie and Alice. They are busy with school and zenana work, and caring for orphans and famishing people."

9. The station at Mahoba was opened in 1894 by Miss Graybiel and Miss Adelaide Gail Frost. They have a bungalow and orphanage,

and are caring for about 70 homeless babies
and motherless girls.   Medical work has also
been undertaken by Dr. Rosa Lee Oxer.   There
is a church of 23 members.   During the famine
a " Children's kitchen " was kept from which,
in 60 days, more than 19,700 meals were given
to little starvelings.   A. McLean says of the
bungalow planned and built by Miss Graybiel:
" It is surrounded by temples, shrines, idols,
sacred trees, old palaces, and suttee mounds.
It is a light in a dark place."

10.   UNITED STATES.—The home work of
the C. W. B. M. has been widely distributed.
Appropriations have been granted from time
to time to various State Societies, and many
cities have been helped, such as Buffalo and
Rochester, in New York; Altoona, Pa.; Roan-
oke, Newport News and Charlottsville, Va.;
Winston, N. C.; Athens, Ga.; Duluth, Minn.;
Sacramento and Santa Barbara, Cal.; Portland,
Ore ; Ogden, Utah ; and West Superior, Wis.
Montana and Colorado, however, have been
looked upon as the special field of this society.
In these two states it has fostered the work
from its beginning.   In Montana the work
was begun in 1882 in Helena and Deer Lodge
by M. L. Streator and Galen Wood respectively.
In that state there are now 16 organized

churches, 12 houses of worship, 3 outposts, 1,052 members, and church property valued at $76,266.00.

In 1890 a mission was started among the Chinese in Portland, Oregon, and Jeu Hawk, a converted Chinaman educated at Des Moines, Iowa, was placed in charge of it. There is now a church of 23 members, a night school with an enrollment of 66, and an average attendance of 24.

11. EDUCATIONAL DEPARTMENT.—In 1892 the Woman's Board undertook the support of a Bible chair in the University of Michigan, at Ann Arbor, by the creation of a special fund. C. A. Young was sent into the field to represent the work, and H. L. Willett was called to the chair. The work has grown steadily from the first, the total receipts having reached $17,149.88, of which $7,900 is endowment. In 1896-7 the enrollment of students in attendance was 130. This is a new movement. Mrs. Burgess, in recommending it at the Nashville Convention, in 1892, said: "No such thing existed the world over." At present Prof. George P. Coler is in charge of the Ann Arbor Bible Chair, and is planning enlargements of the work.

12. At Hazel Green in Wolf County, Ky.,

is the school fondly known as the " Mountain Mission." It is a school of academic grade, and is in charge of Mr. and Mrs. W. H. Cord. The people in this region are very poor, and are correspondingly destitute of educational privileges. Tuitions are placed very low; they amounted, however, last year to $800.co. Many district school teachers attend this school to further equip themselves for work. The enrollment is not far from 200. This is one of the most commendable of missionary enterprises. It was the first mission of the kind in the mountains of Kentucky, but since its beginning 12 have been started by four denominations.

13. Quite recently Monterey, Mexico, has been selected as the location of a mission school, and M. L. Hoblit has been placed in charge of it. Mexico, like many another Spanish, Roman Catholic country, has suffered from illiteracy, from the whole catalogue of Romish idolatries and superstitions, and from political revolutions. It is but a few years since Protestant missionaries were as bitterly persecuted in Mexico as in Spain. But now Mexico is a republic; the Jesuits have been expelled; the estates of the church have been confiscated; and the country is open to Protestant effort.

We shall watch the Monterey mission with great interest.

14. MISSION BANDS.—The C. W. B. M. has no more interesting chapter than that relating to the children. The systematic training of children for mission work was begun in 1884. Children's Bands were organized in many churches, and Mrs. Joseph King, of Allegheny Pa., was chosen as National Superintendent. Within two years the children thus guided and inspired raised $1,700.00 for the Josephine Smith memorial chapel in Akita, Japan (see page 44). From that time till the present they have been enthusiastically engaged in building, and the following is the remarkable list of their achievements:

"In 1887-8 they were working for a bungalow at Bilaspur, India, and a church at Missou'e, Mont.; in 1889, school house and orphanage at Bilaspur; 1890, hospital, Bilaspur; 1891, aiding the General Fund mainly; 1892, furnishing hospital; 1893, school in Kingston; 1894, dormitory in Bilaspur; 1895, bungalow in Bina and enlargement of Chata school in Bilaspur; 1896, bungalow and orphanage in Mahoba, and $1,000 for support of orphans in India; and this year, 1897, for a Mission home at Oberlin and chapel at Torrington, Jamaica, and $5,000 for various buildings in India."

15. In many places Junior Endeavor Societies have taken the place of Mission Bands, but their gifts are being united with those of the Mission Bands, and the work is virtually the same. In several of the states superintendents of this work have been appointed, and Miss Mattie Pounds of Indianapolis is now the National Superintendent. She says that the work has been popular from the beginning. It is the rule that children readily enlist in Christly enterprises. We have now a total of 1146 Mission Bands, Junior Societies, and Intermediate Endeavor Societies. Their offerings in 1896-7 amounted to $10,402.36.

16. From the first this Society has been happy in its union of the educational and the financial phases of missionary work. Not only are offerings made at the monthly meetings, but educational and devotional programmes are presented. Instruction in Missions is constantly kept before the Mission Bands and Junior Endeavor Societies. Additional educational forces are the two publications of the Society, the "*Missionary Tidings*," and "*Junior Builders*," both published at

Indianapolis, and each reaching a circulation of about 12,000.

———

QUESTIONS: 1. When was this Society organized? 2. What leading papers favored it? 3. Who are its present officers? 4. Recall its five particular objects. 5. Through what local societies does it seek to reach these objects? 6. What was its income last year? 7. What was its first mission? 8. What is its policy as regards the training of native workers for Jamaica? 9. How many stations has this Board in India, and what are their names? 10. What equipment have the workers in Bilaspur? 11. What physicians have charge of the medical work in Bilaspur? 12. Who are the missionaries at Bina? 13. Where is Deoghur, and who established the station there? Who are helpers in the work? 14. When was the station at Mahoba opened, and by whom? 15. What states have been the special field of this Society in the United States? 16. Where is the mission among the Chinese, and who has charge of it? 17. What schools are fostered by this Society? 18. What are the religious conditions of Mexico, and in what city has the C. W. B. M. begun a mission? 19. In what ways has the C. W. B. M. succeeded in enlisting the children in missionary work? 20. What distinctive work are the children doing? 21. What is the paper published in their behalf called? 22. How much did they raise last year? 23. What is the leading publication of the C. W. B. M.

CHAPTER XII.

AMERICAN CHRISTIAN MISSIONARY SOCIETY.

President, 1897-'98 ....F. D. POWER, Washington, D. C.
Corresponding Secretary....B. L. SMITH, Cincinnati, Ohio.
Place of business, Cincinnati, Ohio.

1. The object of this society according to Article II of its constitution is to "Spread the Gospel in this and in other lands." Its membership consists of Life Directors, Life Members, Annual Members, and delegates from Churches of Christ, and from States. The payment of $100.00 in five annual installments constitutes a Life Director; of $50.00 in five annual installments, a Life Member; of $5.00 annually, an Annual Member.

2. This is the oldest of our missionary societies. It was organized in Cincinnati, Ohio, in October, 1849, by delegates who came together in response to an informal call. These delegates represented 121 churches and the annual meetings of the following ten states: Indiana, Ohio, Kentucky, Missouri, Illinois, Virginia, Georgia, Michigan, Louisiana, and Pennsylvania. Among them are found many names of the leaders in our great movement for the restoration of primitive Christianity. As early as 1842 Alexander Campbell wrote in the

Millennial Harbinger, "We can do comparatively nothing in distributing the Bible abroad without co-operation. We can do comparatively little in the great missionary field of the world either at home or abroad without co-operation. We cannot concentrate the action of tens of thousands of Israel in any great Christian effort without co-operation." Speaking of the organization of this society the present Corresponding Secretary says finely, "Thus was born the child of twenty-five years of prayerful thought and study of God's will; it was the wisdom of the heroic pioneers of the Restoration."

3. In still further statement of the purpose and spirit of the organization the following points should be noted:

1st. The men who called the Convention and who guided its deliberations were the fathers of our movement. They fully understood the meaning of the movement and they knew the applications and limitations of the motto "Where the Scriptures speak, we speak; where the Scriptures are silent, we are silent."

2nd. Realizing the insufficiency of individual effort and recognizing that the very genius of Christianity leads to brotherliness, and therefore co-operation, in good works, these fathers of our movement sought to promote by united effort the restoration of primitive Christianity.

3rd. There was practical harmony and unanimity in this action, after the fullest and freest discussion.

4th. The men who organized our general missionary work were, with the fewest exceptions, faithful to it to the end of their days.

5th. There was in that Convention the strictest care to not assume any ecclesiastical prerogatives.

6th. Every Convention since has been equally careful to refrain from assuming any authority over the Churches; they are really mass meetings to plan for advancing the missionary enterprise.

To those men the Cause of Missions was the Cause of God; the chief instrumentality in the propagation of the Gospel.

4. Jerusalem was our first Mission field. Dr. Jas. T. Barclay of Virginia offered himself to that first Convention as a foreign missionary and advocated "Zion, the City of the great King" as the most appropriate place for the first mission field of that people who were set for the Restoration of the Old Jerusalem Gospel.

5. An affecting incident in the early work of the Society was the career of Alexander Cross. He was a bright and consecrated negro slave whose freedom was purchased in 1853 by the churches of Christian Co., Kentucky. He offered himself as a missionary to his own race in Africa and was sent out to Liberia by the American Society. The following year he died of the African fever and his name stands first on the roll of our missionary martyrs.

6. The American Christian Missionary Society has been fruitful, notwithstanding the fact that it has always been straitened for means to carry out its gracious designs. Its records show that it has organized 2,184 churches; caused to be raised and expended $1,986,644.00; that never was a dollar of its funds lost through dishonesty; nor was there ever a whisper of scandal about its administration; its missionaries have baptized 84,648 into the Christ; its record is one of the highest honor.

In 1858 Jas. Beardsley was sent to Jamaica and inaugurated the work there so successfully carried on at present by the Christian Womans' Board of Missions.

The Central Church in Chicago is a child of this society, as also the first churches in Philadelphia, Boston, Washington, Minneapolis, Milwaukee, Galveston and a hundred other cities in the United States.

Our Home Board is helping 30 State Boards do mission work within their borders as follows: New England, New York, Eastern Pennsylvania, Maryland, District of Columbia, West Virginia, Virginia, North Carolina, South Carolina, Georgia, Florida, Alabama, Mississippi, Louisiana, Texas, Arkansas, New Mexico, Southern California. Northern California, Oregon, Washington, North Dakota, South Dakota, Nebraska, Kansas, Indian Territory, Oklahoma, Minnesota, Wisconsin, and Michigan.

This help has quickened the work of missions in all these states and has resulted in hundreds being brought into the kingdom of our Lord.

In New England last year the increase as a result of mission work done by our Home Board was 22 per cent.; in New York 17 per cent. In Chicago two new churches have been organized the last three months as a result of its work. This makes seven churches in four years in that city.

7. Every dollar put into the treasury of the Board of Home Missions draws four or five other dollars into the work of the church. It supplements the local efforts and quickens the

liberality of our weak churches to know that
the brotherhood is helping them.

On an average every five dollars spent in
home missions brings a soul into the kingdom
of our Lord, and every three hundred dollars so
spent results in the organization of a church.

On an average three hundred dollars a year
sustains a missionary the entire time in the
home field.

Bequests of five thousand dollars given to
the Home Board are put into a permanent
fund, and the Board agrees to use the interest
to sustain a missionary all the time. Long
after one has entered into rest he can further
the work of our dear Lord by making such
bequests.

By what is known as the Annuity plan, this
society receives moneys upon which it pays
the donors 6 per cent. annually during their
lifetime, the said moneys thereafter becoming
the property of the society.

8. The society has been a prolific mother.
She has given to the church the Christian
Woman's Board of Missions—born at Cincinnati in October, 1874, that splendid agency
which came to the womanhood of our churches
and found them with idle hands and taught
them to work for God in missions.

She likewise gave to the church the Foreign Christian Missionary Society, organized in 1875; and the Board of Church Extension, organized in 1883; and the Board of Negro Evangelization, organized in 1890; and the Board of Education, organized in 1895; and the Board of Ministerial Relief, organized also in 1895.

It is thought by many that in giving place unselfishly to all these Christly organizations the mother society herself has been made to suffer, and that the work of home missions has been measurably neglected, and that now the cry, "Home missions to the front," is imperative.

9. It is to this society that we look year by year for statistical reports of our work as a people. Portions of the report presented at Indianapolis in October, 1897, by the Statistical Secretary, G. A. Hoffman, are reproduced here as being of great interest. The report says:

"The growth of a religious body depends on three things: First, the truth emphasized; secondly, the intelligence, zeal, scholarship and spiritual power of its ministry; thirdly, the thoroughness of its organization. The Christian Church is pre-eminently strong in the first.

It is acknowledged everywhere that the truth which forms the basis of our Zion is wise, acceptable and Scriptural. We have the Christ of the New Testament, Christ the revelation of God, Christ our own and only ideal, our hope and the Savior of men.

Of the second item we may not beable to say as much. It is true that our ministry is of more than average intelligence, and has far more than average zeal. In spirituality and piety it also compares well. But it must not be forgotten that during the last twelve years our churches in America have gained one hundred per cent. During the same twelve years our ministry, in scholarship and numbers, has gained only forty-five per cent. Both of these gains are very large, but our membership has been growing more rapidly than our ministry.

But our greatest need is in more thorough organization for work. The experience of a half century has clearly demonstrated this. Let the work of organization continue until it shall embrace every disciple of our Lord in the work of extending the Master's kingdom. The reports for last year and this are as follows:

	1896.	1897.	GAIN.
Number Churches	9,607	10,029	422
" Communicants	1,003,672	1,051,079	47,407
" Bible schools	6,657	7,284	627
" Scholars and Teachers in B. S.	639,531	676,949	37,418
" Ministers of the Gospel	5,360	5,780	420
Value of church property	$15,805,447	$16,586,677	$781,230

These reports indicate a very commendable gain. The per cent. is from four and one-half to ten.

The missionary reports for the various societies show the following amounts received for the year's work:

Foreign Society	$106.222
Christian Woman's Board of Missions	62,681
American Christian Missionary Society	30,548
Board of Church Extension	27,212
Board of Negro Education and Evangelization	11,364
State Missionary Societies	185,892
Miscellaneous Missions	6,000
Total for Missions	$429,919

. This shows a gain over last year. While this gain may seem small, it is gratifying to know that there is a gain in such times of depression. It shows an offering of forty-three cents per member. This is comparatively good when we consider the relative location of our people and their marvelous growth, with many new and undeveloped members.

10. The Corresponding Secretaries have been fifteen in number,—James Challen 1849-

1850, Thurston Crane 1850–1851, David S. Burnett 1851–1857, also 1861–1863; Chas. Louis Loos 1857, Benjamin Franklin 1857, Isaac Errett 1857–1860, B. W. Johnson 1864, O. A. Burgess 1865, W. C. Rogers 1866, John Shackleford 1867–1868, Thomas Munnell 1868–1877, F. M. Green 1877–1882, R. Moffett 1882–1893, J. H. Hardin, 1893–1895, Benjamin L. Smith 1895 to the present.

Since the last Secretary was called to the office a considerable indebtedness has been met and the work greatly enlarged ; the society is now free from all debts except to love and serve the Church.

11.   The vast fields lying open before the American Society are indicated by the following statements:

FOREIGN POPULATIONS.—Sixteen millions of our population are of foreign birth.   There are thirty different nationalities represented in every American city having a population above 250,000.

In Chicago there are forty thousand Poles gathered in a solid body, half as many Hungarians, and as many Bohemians, in solid masses of ignorance and squalor; having no sympathy or concern for American institutions, save generally a hostile one; no religious attention save that which is rendered oppressive by superstition. These are grounds of grave apprehension for the future. We have 300,000 Italians untouched by Protestant Christianity. In Texas twenty counties are dominated by Germans, an excellent class. There are 300,000 Scandinavians in Minnesota, 1,000,000 in Wisconsin, 100,000 in communities throughout the Dakotas, Kansas and Montana. They need the American church, for the second generation will not go to the church where the services are in their fathers' tongue, since it is rapidly becoming a foreign tongue to them; if they are not saved by the American type of Christianity they become convivial in their habits and drift into infidelity.

The figures show that there are nine million people in the United States who are unable to worship God in the English tongue; the work of reaching these people is simply tremendous, but it must be done if America is to be saved and held for Christ.

In these masses of foreign populations lies the problem of foreign-home missions. They are practically indigestible material if past methods are the most effective that can be employed for their evangelization. Twenty per cent. of our immigrants are under fifteen years of age, half are under twenty-five years.   If we were only ready to take them at this impressible age and Americanize and evangelize them, one element of danger would be eliminated.

12.   MOUNTAIN WHITES.—These people are poor and without any incentives to self-development.   They are without capital, without markets, without railroads, without good highways even; without almost everything but an ardent, universal, all-possessing *want*.   Thousands of young people who are sitting upon fenc:s, or lolling over rickety gates, gazing into a future filled with dim imaginings of what they would be and do, because they have now nothing to do, and do not know how to do anything, would start for school to-morrow if they had the means.   Fifty years will not be time enough to lift up these people and put them into possession of their inheritance.

They present a most promising and interesting field for home mission work; they respond very quickly to the guiding hand of the teacher and preacher; they are a peculiar people, simple in manner, strong in prejudices and devoted to their personal liberties.

13.   CITY EVANGELIZATION.—The largest field for home missions is that of city evangel-

ization.   One-third of the population of the
United States is found in cities; the attrac-
tions of the city, social, intellectual, material,
are winning men away from the more quiet
homes in the country.   Farm machinery has
released thousands of men from the farm labor,
and the inventions of steam and electricity
have opened thousands of doors to men in the
city.

This movement is permanent; there will be
no reaction.   The causes are permanent, and
in the city will be wrought out the problems
of our destiny; there we have the pauper and
the mendicant, the lawless and vicious classes.
Who can describe the depth of suffering, of
degradation, of utter misery in them ?   Poverty, anarchism, socialism, riot—these proclaim
restlessness of soul, and blind groping for
pillars of support.

The church is wiser than all the masters of
social science, for she knows that if she could
bring all these perturbed masses into an experimental knowledge of the saving power of
the Gospel, anarchism would be robbed of its
terrors, intemperance would cease, and a large
part of the poverty, and all the degradation,
would disappear from among us.

14.   NEGRO POPULATION.—Six   million

negroes lift up their hands for help as indicated in another chapter.   This is distinctively a home mission field.

Archdeacon Farrar says: "To be truly great is to see what God is doing, and to do it with Him; for human history flows in a riverbed God has marked out for it."   He that runs counter to this current makes only an eddy, and his life comes to naught.   This element of greatness the Home Missionary Society possesses, for it sees God's plan for the development of the American negro into a positive factor in American national life and material prosperity,and it throws itself into this current, and God's providence has borne it onward in a way that is encouraging to those most familiar with its movements.

15.   OUR RELATIONSHIPS.—Lift up your eyes to the harvest: 38 States that need our help, every city in the United States, the 6,000,-000 negroes in the land needing to be led to the larger conception of life, a foreign population of 16,000,000 that is both a promise and a menace, this is the ripe, rich, inviting field of Home Missions.

We are placed in the midst of this great field as the leaven in the meal.

Eight hundred thousand of our million

members are found in a compact mass in the states of Ohio, Indiana, Illinois, Iowa, Eastern Nebraska, Eastern Kansas, Missouri, Kentucky and Tennessee; all the rest of the United States is full of inviting fields for us. (See frontispiece.)

We have a larger frontier than any other leading religious body in the United States; there is frontier in all four directions; all foreign populations are needing us. With the exception of a little work among the Scandinavians we have not touched this part of the home field.

16. HOME MISSIONS IN FOUR WORDS.— The plea for Home Missions can be made in four words:

1—For the sake of souls; nowhere can we win souls with so little effort and so little cost.

2—For the sake of our plea for Christian Union; nowhere can that plea receive so respectful or so successful a hearing as in America.

3—For the sake of our country; America needs the Gospel of our Lord. Jesus Christ is the only statesman who can solve our problems. Every high motive of patriotism appeals to us to make this land Immanuel's Land.

4—For the sake of our Lord Jesus Christ.

Jesus needs America just as America needs Jesus. God has ordained that Nations should be His witnesses as much as individuals. It is ordained that America shall stand before the nations and bear witness. God wants that testimony to be for righteousness and for the Gospel of the Son of God.

The Anglo-Saxon race is the conquering race; God wants that race to be pure and healthful.

By these four words Home Missions lays claim to our love, our help, and our prayers.

(For much of the substance of this chapter the author is indebted to B. L. Smith, Corresponding Secretary of the Society.)

QUESTIONS: 1. Who is the Corresponding Secretary of this Society, and where is its place of business? 2. What is its object? 3. Describe its basis of membership. 4. When was it organized? 5. What was the attitude of our leading men toward it? 6. How does individual effort compare with co-operative effort in the Lord's work? 7. Does the Society assume ecclesiastical authority? 8. Who was our first missionary martyr? 9. How many churches has this Society organized? 10. How much money has it expended? 11. What Board now carries on the work in Jamaica? 12. In how many states is this Society working? 13. What was the per cent. of increase in New England last year as a result of its work? 14. In what ratio does the money of the Society call out

money for the general work? 15. How much saves a
soul, and how much builds a church? 16. What use
is made of bequests of $5,000.00? 17. Describe the
annuity plan. 18. What societies have sprung from
this one? 19. How many congregations in our brotherhood? 20. How many ministers? 21. How many
communicants? 22. What was the grand total raised
for Missions last year? 23. How many in the United
States are of foreign birth? 24. Describe the foreign
population of Chicago; of Texas; of Minnesota; of
Wisconsin. 25. What elements of danger lie in our
foreign population? 26. Describe the Mountain
Whites. 27. Wherein lies the largest field for Home
Missions? 28. How many millions of negroes need
our help? 29. Where are most of our members
found? 30. What advantage does this give us? 31.
What four reasons can you give for Home Missions?

CHAPTER XIII.

BOARD OF NEGRO EDUCATION AND EVANGEL-
IZATION.

1. Previous to the organization of this
Board in 1890 many of our able and consecrated workers had labored that we might have
a part with other religious bodies in civilizing
and saving the negroes of the United States.
Thomas Munnell, C. E. Ireland, R. Faurot,
Dr. W. A. Belding, Jephthah Hobbs, Verona

Coburn, J. W. Jenkins, and Anna Doyen
should be mentioned among the pioneers in
this cause. They laid the foundations upon
which others have built. Although at the
time the result of their labors seemed small,
yet in many of the Southern States to-day we
find negroes who were trained through their
efforts leading their people to better things.
The new Board came into the heritage of the
experience of these pioneers, all of whom gave
it their most cordial support.

2. In the fall of 1891 at the National Convention held in Allegheny, C. C. Smith was
chosen Corresponding Secretary. This date
marks a favorable epoch in the history of the
work. At the same time Mr. Smith was
elected Secretary of the Southern Christian Institute, a Board necessitated by the holding of
property in the State of Mississippi. The work
of the two Boards is virtually one.

Mr. Smith commenced his work January
1st, 1892, and first made an extended tour of
the South to study the needs of the race, and
the great institutions built by Christian philanthropy for their education. He found in the
front rank of these institutions the one maintained and controlled entirely by negroes, in
Tuskegee, Alabama.

3. Of this great industrial school Booker T. Washington is principal. Over two thousand acres of land, upon which thirty-nine buildings have been erected, belong to the institution. This does not seem like an ordinary school, but rather like a hive of industry. Here over one thousand students are being trained for life's work. Young men are not only gardening, but being taught the best method of gardening; they are not only making brick, but are instructed in practical brick-making; men are not only taking down the trees, but doing it with the most improved machinery and the greatest economy of labor. These trees are taken to their own saw-mill and converted into lumber; then their lumber is taken to their own planing-mill and planed and sized; then to their own factories and made into seats and desks for their own school buildings. The wornout lands of central Alabama are made to yield an abundance of cotton by systematic and inexpensive fertilizing; the cotton then goes to their own gin and from it to their own factory and is made into home-spun, which is made up, by their own hands, into clothes for themselves. Here is found almost an independent world.

At the commencement exercises in Tuskegee the boy who can build the best chimney or make the best box in the presence of the audience carries off the honors. The girl with the bread-tray and the best explanation of bread making receives more applause than the one with a dainty essay, and the young woman with the best notions of housekeeping is more apt to receive an encore than the one who sings a solo. In short this institution is both a school and a training school. It is emphatically industrial, and its influence is being felt in all the homes of Alabama.

4. The President of this beneficent institution was a slave boy when Abraham Lincoln pronounced his emancipation proclamation. Cast out to the world he was taken up by the Hampton Institute and given that which he now gives to others. General Armstrong lives in Booker T. Washington. He says, "If my spending three millions of money at Hampton Institute had only trained Booker T. Washington, I would die content." Thus to create for a race its own leaders is our best possible benefaction.

5. This is precisely the work that the Southern Christian Institute, at Edwards, Miss., aims to do. It is modeled as far as possible on the Tuskegee plan. Its plantation

contains eight hundred acres of land, beautifully situated on the banks of the Big Black River about half way between Jackson and Vicksburg. Through it runs the Meridian and Vicksburg Railway, and near it is the city of Edwards. The eastern end of the plantation is a beautiful, rolling campus, dotted here and there with stately trees trimmed with Spanish moss. The knolls of this campus are now crowned with snow-white buildings. The old "plantation house" enlarged, the school building, in which the work has been carried on so long, the new barn, the shop and printing house and the new college building, together with ten cabins, all in good repair, make a group of buildings which go far toward accommodating a great school.

The new machinery plant is almost ready to be put into operation. Every year some new industry is added.

6. At this Institution boys and girls are given a good education; are taught how to do well the things which they will be called upon to do in life; are made to respect themselves and to respect the rights of others and are shown the dignity of labor. Here they gain new conceptions of liberty and duty and return to the communities whence they

came, honest, industrious, pure, good citizens. The best friends of this work are the white people who live in the vicinity of the school. Professor Lehman and his corps of teachers are treated with great courtesy and respect. One man has offered a hundred acres of land on the opposite side of Edwards to any one who will build a school upon it like the Southern Christian Institute. He says: " The negroes taught at this school are, in every way, made better citizens. They are courteous, they are truthful, they do not contract debts which they cannot pay, they are good farmers and are, in all manner of good living and doing, examples to the negroes in this part of the state. Purely from a business standpoint I want another school like the Southern Christian Institute."

7. In 1889 when J. B. Lehman and wife took charge of the school they had no assistant. Now the work requires the president, a superintendent, a matron and six teachers. J. B Lehman, the president, is capable, wise, industrious, patient, Christ-like, and if he is properly supported he will build up a school which will be to central Mississippi what Booker T. Washington's is to central Alabama.

8. Many are now teaching, in different

parts of the South, sent out from the Southern Christian Institute. One of these, Robert Brooks, has made a marked success. Four years ago he opened a graded school in Lum, Alabama, in an old '' meeting house.'' Now there is a campus of six acres upon which a new and capacious school building has been erected, on which there is no indebtedness. A hundred and twenty pupils were in attendance last year and there were two capable assistant teachers. Toward this work the Board gives only two hundred dollars a year. All the rest of the expense is met by the income from the school and donations from the negroes. The white people of the community are enthusiastic in their praise of both Mr. Brooks and his school. They say the school has practically transformed the whole community.

9. A. J. Thomson has, ever since the formation of the Board, taught a Bible school in Louisville, Kentucky, and has had each year from twenty to thirty pupils. Three years ago he was given an assistant, Octavius Singleton, who was first taught at the Southern Christian Institute and graduated at Hiram, Ohio. The pupils in this school are given a good English education and thorough instruction in the Bible and are also taught how to

tell "the story of the Cross." Pupils who have been educated in this school are now preaching in several different states. We have also been enabled to give a few a higher education at Hiram, Ohio, and to support each year from three to five evangelists in the field. Thus the work widens and deepens, new fields open each year which only a lack of means prevents us from entering.

10. For this good work there was raised last year a total of only $8,105 77. At the Indianapolis Convention last October the Board of Negro Education and Evangelization was reunited with the American Christian Missionary Society in accordance with the following recommendations:

"(1) That separate Boards be maintained for the administration of both works, just as heretofore. (2) That the collections be made one. (3) That with the exception of special funds given to some special purpose, the General Board receive eighty per cent. of the income, and the Board of Negro Education and Evangelization twenty per cent. (4) That we re-establish the office of Associate Secretary of the American Christian Missionary Society, and that the said Associate Secretary be the Corresponding Secretary of the Board of Negro

Education and Evangelization. That the Secretary of the American Christian Missionary Society and the said Associate Secretary act in fullest co-operation and be agents to represent both Boards, and to further the work and interests of both Boards before the churches. (5) That all common expenses shall be met out of the common fund. It is hoped that this plan of union will, by reducing the number of general collections, succeed in enlisting the interest of all our churches more in this work, and result in the advancement of the work of both Boards.''

(For much of the substance of this chapter the author is indebted to C. C. Smith, the Corresponding Secretary of the Board of Negro Education and Evangelization.)

QUESTIONS: 1. When was this Board organized? 2. Who is its present Corresponding Secretary? 3. When was he chosen? 4. What did he first do? 5. Upon what school is the Southern Christian Institute modeled? 6. Who is Booker T. Washington? 7. What are the aims of the Tuskegee school? 8. Where is the Southern Christian Institute? 9. How much land does it own? 10. Describe its buildings. 11. What kind of an education does it seek to give? 12. Who is in charge of it? 13. What other schools have we for negroes? 14. How much was raised for this work last year? 15. What action was taken at Indianapolis?

CHAPTER XIV.

CHURCH EXTENSION.

President ....DAVID O. SMART.
Treasurer.............................T. R. BRYANT.
Corresponding Secretary........G. M. MUCKLEY.

Place of business, Kansas City, Mo.

1. Church extension is an exceedingly business like and helpful department of our home missionary work. The enterprise was begun in 1888 under the direction of the American Christian Missionary Society, and is a department of the work of that Society. (The fund was established in 1883, and was in the hands of a committee of the American Society until the organization of the Board above indicated in 1888.) The great need of such a movement is shown by the astonishing fact that nearly thirty-three per cent. of our churches are without church buildings. A recent statement of the Secretary informs us that there are 2,500 such homeless churches. They are found, for the most part, in the growing West and the New South. Little bands of consecrated and enterprising Christians have organized themselves into churches in multitudes of promising places, and are not able to bear much more than the burden of current ex-

penses. Some of them are fostered by State Societies. They meet in homes and halls and school houses, and various kinds of rented rooms. Almost invariably they look forward to a time when they shall be able to build, and enter with joy into their own homes. Hundreds of them would be able and glad to build at once if they could have the help of their brethren in the way of loans of a few hundred dollars at a low per cent. This is precisely the help that the Board of Church Extension gives. A few statements from the Corresponding Secretary of the Board will make the matter quite clear.

2. "The fund was organized because of the need, especially in the West and South and in the suburban wards of Eastern cities. The idea was to stop indiscriminate appeals, and to help by loans instead of sinking money in gifts. Money is loaned to missions in older states when it cannot be borrowed on the ground. This fund is a financial friend to the struggling mission that has no friend financially.

"The fund is loaned for five years to be paid back to the Board in five equal annual installments. It is paid sooner if the mission wishes to do so. Four per cent. interest is charged to cover the current expenses of securing and managing the fund.

"The money is loaned only on first mortgage security, with all other debts paid in cash except what the loan will pay, and the building must be completed to avoid all liens. The mission is therefore out of debt in the town where it is located and is on its way to success."

3. Within ten years there have been 1,500 appeals to this Board for aid. Only about twenty-five per cent. of the calls can be answered. Up to October, 1897, 382 churches had been helped to complete their buildings. The fund now aggregates $156,000.00, and is loaned to 285 congregations. In principal and interest above $90,000 00 has been paid back by the churches to the Board. Money is no sooner paid back than it is again loaned, and it is thus kept constantly at work building houses of worship in needy and promising places. This is an admirable feature of its management, and should commend it to consecrated business men who desire the assurance that their means will go on doing good after they have ceased to direct it.

4. A helpful feature of the work of the Board of Church Extension is its "Named

Loan Funds." These are funds received and administered in the name of the donors or persons designated by them. Such a fund must consist of not less than $5,000.00, to be paid at once or in annual subscriptions through a series of not more than fifteen years. No part of the interest of such funds is used for the expenses of the Board, but goes immediately to the increase of the fund, and is practically compounded semi-annually. Thus used the claim is made for it that it more than doubles its working power in five years.

5. According to a recommendation made at the National Convention in Indianapolis in 1897 an effort is being made to raise the fund to a quarter of a million of dollars by the close of the year 1900.

The Corresponding Secretary of the Board is the editor of a monthly publication entitled *Business and Christianity*, which is devoted to the interest of the enterprise.

———

QUESTIONS: 1. What per cent of our churches are without church buildings? 2. How many houseless churches have we? 3. What is the object of the Church Extension Society? 4. On what conditions does the Society loan money? 5. How many appeals has this Board received in ten years? 6. What per cent of them can it answer? 7. What does the fund now aggregate? 8. What does the Board hope to make it by the year 1900? 9. How many churches are now being helped by it? 10. What is meant by "Named Loan Funds?" 11. How is the interest of such funds used? 12. In how many years does it double its working power? 13. Who are the present officers of this society? 14. What is the name of its monthly publication?

CHAPTER XV.

BOARD OF MINISTERIAL RELIEF.

This Board was organized at Dallas in October, 1895, upon presentations made by A. M. Atkinson in an address in which he set forth the needs, the purpose, and the plan of the work. Its objects as stated in the second annual report made at Indianapolis last Oc'ober is,

"To make suitable provision for the better care of our old and disabled preachers and those who serve and suffer with them, the widows and helpless orphans of deceased preachers, our missionaries in this and foreign lands who through misfortune will need a helping hand."

The receipts the first year were $5,840.45,

of which $1,140.70 was paid out in relief.
The receipts of the second year were $12,064.40,
of which $3,173.50 was paid out in relief.   At
the time of the last report 133 persons had
been helped from this fund, 77 of them during
the last year, as follows; 25 preachers and
their wives, 17 widows of worthy preachers,
and ten children whose fathers died young
leaving their families destitute and deeply
afflicted.

The plan of the Board is to use 25 per
cent. of the current receipts for relief, and to
reserve 75 per cent. as a permanent fund the
interest of which only can be used.   Many
worthy but neglected and suffering servants
of Christ have been reported, and the present
beneficiaries are found in many of the states
from ocean to ocean.   Touching letters are
often received by the secretary showing how
the help has relieved distress keener than
hunger.

In addition to the above ministries the
Board during the last year incurred the funeral
expenses of six preachers, three of whom were
above 80 years of age, and one widow who
was 85.   Two of these brethren had given
sixty years to the ministry; one had sacrificed
a competency in order to continue in the work,

and was at last obliged to receive partial support from the county fund; all were great sufferers. "Is it not," says the report, "a beautiful memory that the closing days of these faithful servants of God were brightened by the grace of this sacred ministry?"

The fund is administered after careful investigation and in accordance with a set of rules that protect it against fraudulent or unworthy beneficiaries. Almost without exception the present recipients are devout and uncomplaining sufferers, who have not so much as asked for help, but who have been found out by or reported to the secretary.

Mr. Atkinson himself, who is a Christly business man living in Wabash, Indiana, has given $6,000 to this fund. He has also traveled extensively in its advocacy among our churches. He thoroughly realizes that he is thus engaged in a holy ministry. It is to be regretted that he has reached that period in life where by reason of increasing years and infirm health he is no longer able to continue this beneficent work. Recently therefore it was announced that D. R. Lucas of Indianapolis, a preacher widely and favorably known among us, had been chosen to succeed him as Corresponding Secretary of the Board.

One of the sources of income to this fund deserves special emphasis. Preachers actively engaged in the ministry are asked for $2.00 each annually as an offering to it. Mr. Atkinson in his last report makes the following appeal to preachers: "You are strong now, but the shadows may soon fall upon you, when you too may need a helping hand. Your attitude toward this ministry should no longer remain uncertain. Your indifference will be cruel, your neglect unpardonable. You surely desire to have fellowship with your fellow preachers in their affliction."

CHAPTER XVI.

THE EDUCATIONAL BOARD.

This also, like the Boards of Ministerial Relief, Church Extension, and Negro Evangelization, is under the auspices of the American Christian Missionary Society. It is devoted to "the threefold policy of (1) publishing reports, statistics and general educational information; (2) arranging for and holding one educational conference each year; (3) securing speakers on our educational work for our State and National Conventions."

This Board attempts to raise no funds, but receives such voluntary offerings as are placed in its charge to defray the expenses of the publication, quarterly, of *The Educational Bulletin*. Its work is distinctively that of agitation by way of the printing of statistics, the publication of addresses on education, and disseminating general educational literature.

The annual Educational Conference, held under its auspices, seeks "the co-ordination of the interests of all the colleges, so that they stand together on important questions, and not as representing the isolated interests of isolated schools." It aims to do in the realm of education what organization does in any other field. It was through the initiative taken by this Board that a Bible school has been established in connection with Butler College. Of this school Jabes Hall, formerly a well known pastor in the cities successively of Cleveland, Ohio, and Richmond, Virginia, is the dean.

The president of the Educational Board is E. V. Zollars, president of Hiram College, Ohio, and the secretary is Mrs. Albertina Allen Forrest, of Irvington, Indiana.

CHAPTER XVII.*

RELIGIOUS CONDITIONS IN ENGLAND.

1. The religious impediments to our work in England are, first, the Romanizing tendency of the Established Church; secondly, Rationalistic science and criticism; thirdly, lack of definite Scriptural teaching among Nonconformists, except upon a few points of distinctive difference with the Establishment.

In the Church of England there are three lines of cleavage, the Evangelical section, the Broad Church, and the High Church. The first is the best, but it is feeble and singularly lacking in leadership. The Broad Church is strong in intellect and culture, but weak in numbers and spirituality. The High Church is far in the lead in point of numbers, wealth, social prestige, organization, and men of genius. It embraces the ritualistic and Romanizing

---

*An adequate presentation of our foreign fields cannot be given without some reference to their respective religions. It is hoped that these closing chapters will help the student to realize the moral and religious conditions that confront our foreign missions. Though the matter is terse, considering the subjects treated, the author has aimed at precision and justice.

party. About 4,000 of its clergy, including many suffragan bishops, belong to the English Church Union, which aims at the so-called re-union with Rome. There are about 7,000 of these Romanizing Anglican clerics, re-enforced by 3,000 Jesuit priests occupying Anglican pulpits in disguise. In many English churches the mass is celebrated just as in Roman Catholic churches, though at the most solemn moment of their lives the English clergy sign a declaration that they regard the mass as a "blasphemous fable." The veneration of the cross, the elevation of the host, auricular confession, priestly absolution, prayers for the dead, Maryolatry, conversion of bread and wine into the body and blood of Jesus, along with other Papal errors and idolatries, are openly taught and practiced within the pale of the Established Church by traitors to Protestantism who swear allegiance to its principles in their ordination vows. These same priests pour the virus of sacerdotalism into the blood of the children of England in the public schools at the expense of the tax payers.

2. Against Statechurchism and priest-craft, Nonconformity is the hope of England. The Wesleyans, Presbyterians, Congregationalists, Baptists, and several small bodies of

people that do not conform to the Establishment, are known as Nonconformists, or "dissenters," and "dissent" to the church imagination is the incarnation of all that is vulgar and mean. In most of the villages and rural districts, to be known as a dissenter, is to be ostracized from society and boycotted in business. Most of the intolerance and bigotry of England are found in the state religion, engendered as much by the social caste spirit, as by religious exclusiveness and ecclesiastical pride. Denominational lines are loosely and indistinctly drawn in the Nonconformist churches. There is more spiritual unity in these bodies than can be found anywhere else, perhaps, in the world. One church is esteemed about as good as another, barring the Anglican and Roman Catholic. The widespread appreciation of spiritual and fundamental unity, and the comparative freedom from denominational bigotry, are points in favor of New Testament Christianity, but the general indifference to distinctive religious teaching, except on points of difference between Conformity and Nonconformity, constitutes a serious hindrance.

3. The characteristic of Anglicanism is devotion to an institution. The characteristic of Nonconformity is devotion to a principle and

to the personality of its leaders. Institutionalism
has in it the element of permanency and self-per-
petuity, and depends little on either principles or
persons for its success.   The Nonconformist
principle is religious freedom and the spirituality
of the Gospel, over against the church doctrine
of magic rites and a supernatural priesthood.
In the absence of visible forms and institutions
on which to lean, it is natural that the Nonconformist should be profoundly influenced by
the personality of the preacher and leader who
embodies the principle in which he believes.
England's great need of our Christological
teaching is seen in the fact that it combines
devotion to principles, personality, and divine
institutions without wresting either out of its
proper place in the system of truth.

(The author is indebted for the substance of this
chapter to J. J. Haley, formerly pastor at Birkenhead,
England.)

———

QUESTIONS: 1. Name the impediments to our
work in England. 2. How many sections in the
Established Church? 3. Which is the Romanizing
party? 4. How many of the Anglican clergy belong
to the Romanizing party? 5. What Romish rites are
practiced in many English churches? 6. What is
the hope of England? 7. What is the character of the
denominationalism among Nonconformists? 8. What

are the leading distinctions between Anglicanism and Nonconformity? 9. Why is our presentation of the Gospel especially adapted to England's needs?

CHAPTER XVIII.

HINDUISM.

1. The Hindus are our cousins. They and we belong to the great Aryan or Indo-European race. Because of this their religious teaching and condition must have for us an unusual interest. Enough may be said of it, we trust, in a few pages to enable the student to appreciate in a goodly degeee the position of our Christian missionaries in India.

2. The most ancient of the sacred books of the Hindus are the Vedas. In a general way they may be classified as Hymns, Brahmanas, and Upanishads, and they represent the most ancient worship of the Aryans. To them nearly everything in nature, the sun, the moon, the wind, the rivers, the earth, the sea, was the manifestation of a god whose good graces might be won by gifts, or who might be angry and very ugly if he was not well paid for being good. The Brahmanas are ritualistic, and the Upanishads philosophical. The

Rig-Veda consists of 1028 hymns, all of them as old as the Psalms of David, many of them older. Being handed down from generation to generation they came to have the force of revelation. They contain no definite system of belief, and inculcate now the worship of one god, and then another, and still another, as supreme. In one hymn it is Agni, or fire; in another, Surya, or the sun; in another, Indra, or the rain; in another, Vishnu, the preserver, or Siva, the destroyer, who is celebrated as the god of gods. Nothing could more forcibly show the indefinite teaching of the Vedas than the fact that pantheism, polytheism, monotheism, tritheism, and henotheism have all been deduced from them.

3. Other writings of Hinduism are the Shastras, containing rules for everyday life, for the regulation of castes, and the constitution of society; the Ramayana and the Maha-Bharata, epic poems, treating of the deeds of the heroes Rama and Krishna, who in process of time were deified and worshipped as incarnations of Vishnu; later in production, and last to be named, the Puranas and the Tantras, devoted to the worship of the female energy of certain gods, especially Siva. According to best authorities they are "insuffer-

ably long and wearisome, and the Tantras are often grossly immoral."

4. On its philosophical side Hinduism is absolutely pantheistic; on its popular side it is grossly polytheistic. It teaches that "there is but one being and no second." This, which they named Brahma, "is the only really existing essence, the one eternal germ of all things, and it delights in infinite expansion, in infinite manifestation of itself, in infinite creation, dissolution and recreation, through infinite varieties and diversities of operation." "Brahma by meditation gave existence to the waters and to a productive seed, which developed into a golden egg, and from that egg he was born as Brahma, the creator of all things."

5. As all things proceed from Brahma, and are Brahma, it follows that all must return to Brahma. The search after God resulted in the identification of the souls of all living things with God, or rather Brahma, and must end according to the teaching of the Upanishads with the absorption of all souls in God, just as the dewdrop glides into the sea. All finite being must be lost in the infinite. All that seems to be is but illusion, and our seeming existence is the root of evil. To be rid of existence is to be rid of evil, but this can only

come by enlightenment, and enlightenment comes by way of transmigration. When by endless rebirths we reach that point where we cut ourselves off from all desire, and recognize our absolute identity with the infinite all—then we fall back into that infinite all, and transmigration ceases. This is the goal of wisdom.

6. Strangely enough, as was said above, Hinduism is also polytheistic. India's gods are reckoned at 330,000,000. Any imaginable thing may be worshipped, but the two gods that come nearest to receiving the worship of all India are Ganesa and the cow. Ganesa is the son of Siva and Parvati, and is worshipped more than his father and mother. He is by some called "lord of the deamon hosts," and he is the god of all new undertakings. He is pot-bellied, sits cross-legged, and has the head and trunk of an elephant. "His hideous image, chiseled in stone, carved in wood and ivory, cast in copper and brass, is found everywhere." Sir Monier Williams says, "I verily believe that the religion of most of the Hindus is simple demonolatry. Men and women of all classes, except perhaps those educated by ourselves, are perpetually penetrated with the idea that from the cradle to the grave they are being pursued and persecuted not only by de-

structive demons but by simple, mischievous imps and spiteful goblins.   This in my opinion is the true explanation of the universal worship of Ganesa."

7.   The worship of the cow is so widespread that it lacks but little of being the one common bond among the Hindus.   There are families that keep a cow simply to worship her. Monkeys are also worshipped, and snakes, and crocodiles, and in short every living thing, for from the standpoint of pantheism and transmigration all life is sacred.   It is thus that polytheism reconciles itself to pantheism.   It is estimated that 20,000 people die in India annually from snake bites, the people fearing to kill snakes because they are sacred.

8.   Hinduism has no message of righteousness for its devotees.   It is lacking entirely in the sublime appeal of Jehovah through Moses to Israel, "Be ye holy for I am holy."   Its tendency is to degrade, for men become like the gods they worship.   Rajah Ramohun Roy is quoted as saying, "Idolatry as now practiced by my countrymen must be looked upon with great horror by common sense as leading directly to immorality and destructive of social comforts.   Every Hindu who devotes himself to this absurd worship constructs for that pur-

pose a couple of male and female idols, some-
times indecent in form, as representing his
favorite deities. There can be but one opinion
respecting the moral character to be expected
of a person who has been brought up with
sentiments of reverence for such beings.'' It
is indeed significant that in proportion as cows
are worshipped women are degraded, and that
in the temples where priests pay their devotions
to monkeys helpless and misguided women are
kept for immoral purposes. Their condition
is condoned by calling them the wives of the
gods. To-day in India as in Palestine when
Jeroboam and Ahab reigned men fashion their
idols after their own gross imaginations,

"Gods changeful, passionate, unjust,
  Whose attributes are rage, revenge, and lust."

9. The system of caste that prevails in
India is a part of the religious system. Among
the sacred books the Dharma-Shastras contain
the rules regulating castes. The very basis of
society is laid in the caste system, the person
being rigidly fixed forever, even in his transmigrations, to the caste in which the Supreme
Lord first placed him. To a high-caste Hindu
there can be no greater calamity than to break
his caste, for then he becomes an outcast.

"That the human race might be multiplied
Brahma caused the Brahmins to spring from
his mouth, the Kshatriyas from his arm, the
Vaisyas from his thigh, and the Sudras from
his feet." Aside from these chief castes there
are numberless minor divisions for every calling in life. No one can ascend. The son of a
Sudra or farmer must ever be a farmer, the son
of a Kshatriya or soldier must be a soldier.
The system forbids brotherliness; it creates ar-
bitrary and impassible barriers, and it precludes progress. A missionary says: "I have
known a Brahmin to die in sight of food placed
there for his sustenance because it had been
cooked by a person of a lower caste. Better
die, he said, and gain heaven, than eat that
food and lose caste, and lose heaven."

10. The chief points in which Hinduism
is at variance with Christianity may be stated
as follows:

1st. Christianity brings us into the presence of a personal God and Creator, who is at
once Father and Friend. It thus forbids pantheism on the one hand, and polytheism with
its gross idolatries on the other, all of which
Hinduism has.

2nd. Christianity presents an absolutely
holy God as revealed in the sinless Savior;

Hinduism has a multitude of negatively good, or absolutely unclean gods.

3rd. Christianity weds conduct to creed in a way that is absolute and imperative. The faith of the Hindu does not affect his conduct unless to degrade it.

4th. Christianity, concerning itself with conduct, appeals to the conscience; Hinduism has no such appeal.

5th. Christianity calls to repentance and offers forgiveness; transmigration with its accompanying karma, or doctrine of consequences, precludes repentance, forgiveness, and conversion.

6th. Christianity offers us a conscious and blissful future life; Hinduism offers us unconsciousness and absorption in the infinite as the goal of attainment after many sad rebirths.

7th. Christianity teaches us that all are brothers, actually in blood, potentially in spirit and conduct; Hinduism builds the unbrotherly barriers of caste.

———

QUESTIONS: 1. What is the ancient stock of the Hindus and ourselves? 2. What are the Vedas? What are their divisions? 3. Name some of the objects of devotion that belong to the Nature-worship of the Vedas. 4. Wherein do the Vedas differ from the Bible as regards the teaching of one supreme God? 5.

Name five other classes of the sacred writings of the Hindus. 6. What is the character of the Shastras? Of the Ramayana and Maha-Bharata? Of the Puranas and the Tantras? 7. Describe Hinduism on its philosophical and its popular sides. 8. According to the Upanishads whence do all things proceed, and whither do they return? 9. Is existence real or illusory? 10. What is the root of evil? 11. How is existence to be gotten rid of? 12. How many gods has India? 13. Name two leading objects of the popular worship. 14. What is the effect of Hindu idolatry upon Hindu morality? 15. What are the relative positions of the cows and the women of India? 16. What is the basis of society in India? 17. Does Hinduism foster or forbid castes? 18. What is the effect of caste upon society and progress? 19. Recall at least seven cardinal points in which Hinduism is in contrast with Christianity.

CHAPTER XIX.

CONFUCIANISM.

1. Confucius was born 551 years before Christ. For 24 centuries he has been the teacher of the multitudinous generations of China. None but a great man could so hold his influence over a nation through tens of centuries. Many of his precepts are eminently wise.

He was not a prophet, but a historian. He was not a revealer, but a compiler. He claimed no message from heaven, but sought to formulate the wisdom of earth. He distinctly repudiates the position of a religious teacher by saying, '' We cannot as yet perform our duties to men; how can we perform our duties to spirits? We know not as yet about life; how can we know about death? My prayers were offered up long ago.''

2. Confucius edited the sacred books (or Kings) of the Chinese, and this was his greatest work. These have been designated in English terms as the Book of Changes, the Book of Odes, the Book of History, the Book of Rites, and the Spring and Autumn Annals. Other books held in great reverence are the Conversations of Confucius, the Book of Filial Piety, the Works of Mencius, and rituals and commentaries, the whole making a vast literature. The sacred books themselves, aside from the commentaries are in volume about as large as the Old Testament.

3. Rev. Arthur H. Smith, author of "Chinese Characteristics," reckons six essential elements of Confucianism, five of which, he says, differentiate it from any other system of non-Christian thought.

1st.   It teaches "the direct responsibility of the sovereign to Heaven, Shang Ti, or God." The Emperor alone worships Shang Ti. Many of the people dimly and idolatrously worship "heaven and earth," but not because Confucius taught them so.

2nd.   Strangely enough Confucianism teaches that the people are of more importance than the sovereign, for he reigns by heaven's decree, and if he loses that he has no right to reign, but the people have a right to rebel. The government therefore amounts to "a despotism tempered by the right of rebellion."

3rd.   It teaches five social relations, those of sovereign and subject, of parents and children, of husbands and wives, of elder and younger brothers, and of friends toward one another.

4th.   It teaches five virtues, namely, benevolence, righteousness, propriety, knowledge, and good faith.

5th.   The force of example, or the presentation of "an ideal or princely man as the model on which every Confucianist should form his character."

6th.   Filial piety, or the worship of ancestors.

Confucius had not half measured the hu-

man heart when he refused to give the people
a religion. Good conduct and good government are not enough, and they are not possible to a Godless people. Humanity refuses
to live perpetually on its own dead level. The
soul may mistake philosophy for religion, but
it must have its flights above the flesh.

4. So myriads of people turned to Lao-
Tse, a philosopher contemporary with Confucius, and from him they sought spiritual help.
He taught the half religious system of the
Tao, a strange mingling of the philosophy of
the absolute, utilitarian morality, and the
magical worship of spirits. Confucius tried
for twenty years to understand Lao-Tse and
could not. He gave it up, saying, "I know
how birds can fly, how fishes can swim, how
beasts can run. The runner, however, may
be snared, the swimmer may be hooked, the
flier may be shot with an arrow. But there is
a dragon; I cannot tell how he mounts on the
wind through the clouds and rises to heaven.
To-day I have seen Lao-Tse, and can only
compare him to the dragon."

The people, however, were not so careful
about understanding Taoism. It was perhaps
the more acceptable to them because of its
mysteries and magic and selfish morality.

They accepted it side by side with Confucianism and found no difficulty in being at the same time Taoist and Confucianist.

5.   The religious condition of China cannot be fully told without naming her Buddhism also.   (See chapter on Buddhism).   This religion was, so Prof. Smith above quoted says, "Invited to China by an emperor more than six hundred years after the birth of Confucius, and it attempted to fill the void in the human heart which longs for salvation and a savior.   The success of this misty and chameleon faith among the millions of hard-headed, practical Chinese has been phenomenal.   For ages Confucianism was its bitter foe, but as a matter of fact these three discordant contradictories have been interblended in a way perhaps elsewhere unexampled on this earth.   Temples are found all over the empire in which the founders of the 'three religions' stand side by side, and by perpetual repetition for several hundred years the maxim that the three doctrines are one has come to be almost as much believed as the doctrines themselves."

6.   From the standpoint simply of secular wisdom Confucius may be called the Solomon of his people.   Though he has stood the test of so many centuries his system has proved

mournfully non-progressive, and it is failing completely as it comes into competition with Christian teaching and civilization. "Confucianism is a spent force. Its golden age is in the past, while the outlook of every Christian land is toward the morning dawn of a bright future."

7. As contrasted with Christianity, Confucianism is deficient at many points.

1st. It is not a revelation and does not claim to be a religion.

2nd. It has no personal God; it cannot therefore offer a divine Fatherhood reaching out man-ward, or a human childhood reaching up God-ward. It does not so much as permit the people to worship its vague Shang Ti, or heavenly state.

3rd. It makes no account of sin, teaches no repentance, offers no forgiveness, and has no Savior. Hence it has no appeal to concience.

4th. Its reverence for parents has become the worship of ancestors, so that the list of a man's grandfathers is the directory of his gods. This necessitates polytheism and vetoes progress, for the worship of one's fathers means the revering of their customs, the turning of the face to the past, and the frowning upon change and innovation.

5th. Still further; the worship of ancestors leads to inordinate self-esteem, in many cases to polygamy, always and everywhere to the practical slavery of the child to the father so long as he lives.

6th.   The godlessness of the three commingled religions of the Chinese have left their votaries a prey to many harmful superstitions. The knowledge of the true God is the only conservative against false gods, and demons, and fiends.   "Having no God men betake themselves to ghosts."

QUESTIONS: 1. When was Confucius born? 2. Did he claim to be more than a man? 3. As a man how does he rank among men? 4. Did he consider himself a religious teacher? 5. What was his greatest work? 6. According to the teachings of Confucus to whom is the emperor responsible? 7. Who are of more importance than the sovereign? 8. What worship, if any, did Confucius teach? 9. Wherein was his great failure? 10. To whom did the people turn for religious help? 11. What other religion has China? 12. Do the Chinese find any difficulty in embracing three systems at the same time? 13. As to vitality and the outlook for the future what are the relative positions of Confucianism and Christianity? 14. In how many vital points is Confucianism deficient? 15. What is the only conservative against idolatry?

CHAPTER XX.

BUDDHISM.

1. Of this religion Sir Monier Williams says, "It passes from apparent atheism and materialism, to theism polytheism, and spiritualism. It is, under one aspect, pessimism; under another, pure philanthropy; under another, monastic communism; under another, high morality; under another, a variety of materialistic philosophy; under another, simple demonology; under another, a mere farago of superstitions, including necromancy, witchcraft, idolatry, and fetishism."

2. In treating of a system so chameleon-like great caution is needed, and a few bold outlines must suffice.

Buddhism, like Christianity, has a personal founder, but unlike Christianity it has no personal savior. Its exhortation to the sufferer imprisoned in all but endless rounds of transmigration is to effect his own escape.

Buddhism, like Christianity, recognizes suffering, but unlike Christianity it does not recognize the exceeding sinfulness of sin. The suffering it seeks to relieve is due to existence itself, and the evil it seeks to avert is transmigration, or the perpetuation of existence.

3. Unlike Christianity Buddhism has no God, though it tolerates gross idolatries, and Buddha himself is worshipped by myriads of people. Having no God it lacks by necessity the Christian teaching of the Fatherhood of God, and consequently also the true basis for the teaching of the brotherhood of man.

Unlike Christianity Buddhism has no heaven, and so far from seeking a future existence of bliss it seeks the end of existence. "Christianity demands the suppression of selfishness; Buddhism demands the suppression of self. In the one the true self is elevated; in the other it is annihilated." "What shall I do to inherit eternal life?" says the Christian. "What shall I do to inherit eternal extinction of life?" says the Buddhist.

4. At the heart of Christianity lies love, leading to brotherliness and self-sacrifice, and ultimately to the highest possible worship of a lovable God and Father. At the heart of Buddhism lies the doctrine of merit, leading to selfishness. The good deeds of the Buddhist look toward the purchasing of merit; his merit affects his karma, or fate, and his karma determines his transmigrations, or the extinction of them.

5. Christianity is a revelation; Buddhism

is an invention. Christianity speaks with authority and is final; Buddhism simply exhorts and is experimental. Christianity fills the soul with love and God, and thus precludes idolatry; Buddhism being loveless and Godless leaves a vacancy that the soul seeks to fill by gross and numberless idolatries.

6. As contrasted with the authentic account of the life of Jesus the accounts of the life of Buddha are legendary; nevertheless they are highly interesting. For the following the author is indebted to George T. Smith, a returned missionary from Japan: At the foot of the Himalayas lived the tribe of Sakyas, and the Aryan clan. To their king was born a son, Siddartha Gautama. This was before Christ, 1027, according to northern Buddhists; 622 B. C., according to southern annals. This was not his first appearance on earth. In numerous forms of animals and birds, and as man in various conditions of life, he had been on the earth 550 times.

7. The early years of Gautama are enshrouded in the legendary and the miraculous. From the heaven called Tushita he descended in the form of a white elephant that he might be born the last time. At his birth there were found on his body the 32 marks and 80 forms

of beauty whose presence betoken a Buddha, that is, an enlightened one. He far surpassed other boys in studies, in athletics, and in archery. At ten, tradition says, he tossed an elephant over the walls. His father, who was the Rajah or King of Kapilivastu, concealed from him all sickness and sorrow and death. At seventeen he was married to his cousin Yasodhara, to whom he had been married in many previous states of existence, once when both were peasants dwelling in the woods, and once when both were finest tigers of the jungle. At twenty-nine he left his wife and child and palace, and wandered away to be a monk of the Sakya tribe, hence his name Sakya—Muni.

8. He was now a mendicant, pledged to chastity and poverty, clothed in a yellow robe, and begging his daily ration of rice. The occasion of this was that four visions appeared to him; a decrepit old man tottering on his staff, a leper writhing in pain, a decomposing corpse, and lastly a mendicant seeking escape from the ills of life. Reflecting upon these things disgust with life came over him, and awaking at midnight, and finding the dancing girls of the palace asleep, he passed out. He longed to take his boy in his arms, but the

mother's arm was on the babe's head, and he refrained. For a distance his faithful chari- oteer, Channa, attended him; but Buddha sent him back to say to his father that he would not return till he had become a Buddha. Cut- ting off his hair, and exchanging his royal robes for the dress of a mendicant, he plunged into the wilderness, a penniless student and a homeless wanderer. For six years he devoted himself to intense meditation, ceaseless vigils, and painful penances. He sought Brahmanical teachers, but they gave him no light. His austerities and self-mortifications did not bring him peace and deliverance. At last in despair, having reduced his ration of rice to one grain a day, he threw himself under the shade of a pipal tree, now called the Bo tree or tree of wisdom. Here he spent forty days and nights assailed by the severest temptations of the powers of evil, till at last the light came to him; he became a Buddha; renounced his penances, and went forth as a preacher of the new and noble, eight-fold way of wisdom. For forty- five years in the valley of the Ganges he preached, dying calmly among his friends at the age of eighty. His last exhortation to Ananda, his cousin and favorite disciple, was this: "O Ananda, I am growing old, and full of years, and my journey is drawing to its close. I have reached eighty years—my sum of days—and just as a worn-out cart can only with much care be made to move along, so my body can only be kept going withdifficulty. It is only when I become plunged in meditation that my body is at ease. In future, be ye to yourselves your own light, your own refuge; seek no other refuge. Hold fast to the truth as your lamp. Hold fast to the truth as your refuge; look not to anyone but yourself as a refuge."

His last exhortation to his followers was, "Behold now, O monks, I exhort you—every-thing that cometh into being passeth away; work out your own perfection with diligence."

9. The doctrinal basis of Buddhism is the Four Noble Truths held by all Buddhist sects. These verities are:

1. Suffering exists wherever sentient being exists.
2. The cause of suffering is desire, for either pleasure or existence. This leads to rebirth, and rebirth is suffering.
3. Deliverance from suffering can be effected only by the complete cessation of desire. This is Nirvana. Some make it extinction of being. Others, absorption in the infinite.
4. Nirvana can be attained only by walking in the Way of Buddha or the Noble Eight Fold Path.

(1) Right views, (as to the nature and cause of suffering).

(2) Right thoughts.

(3) Right words.

(4) Right actions.

(5) Right means of livelihood. That is as a mendicant, living in celibacy and on offered alms.

(6) Right application of the spirit to the study of the law.

(7) Right memory, or freedom from error in recollecting the law.

(S) Right meditation.

The last four apply to the monks; the first four to laymen as well as monks. He who travels the Eight Fold Path passes four stages: Having entered upon the "stream of holy conduct" he escapes from self-delusion, doubt, and reliance on rites. Next, lust, hatred and delusion are reduced to a minimum and the devotee is a saint. He is now subject to but one more rebirth. In the third stage sensuality and self will are extinguished; then he enters upon the fourth, where he escapes from all error and desire.

On this basis an elaborate system has been established. Temples, priests, rites, incense, and superstitions abound.

10. Buddhism has eight hells (some say a thousand), each painted as vividly as Dante's one, but it has no heaven. Nirvana is one of

the key words of Buddhism, and takes the place in that system that heaven does in Christian teaching. It denotes the end of transmigration, the last of rebirths, the cessation of conscious being, the exhaustion of one's Karma, or as said above, absorption in the infinite.

11. In India Buddhism arose in direct opposition to the Hindu system of caste, proclaiming equality, and in this respect anticipating Christianity. But in a few centuries its votaries became enervated and corrupt. The self-conquest and universal charity which won for it numerous adherents became too difficult as the system became popular. It grew in its native land till about 400 A. D., then declined for about four centuries, when a great persecution arose and it was driven out completely. Its effects are manifest in the resultant Hinduism of to-day, but there is not a Buddhist in India.

12. The Buddhist countries are Ceylon, Burmah, and Siam in the south; and China, Thibet, Corea, and Japan in the north. These countries comprise a population of about 450,-000,000 of people, but it would be far from correct to estimate them all as Buddhists, for in not one of these countries is Buddhism the sole religion.

Twelve sects of Buddhists survive out of thirty in Japan. Some are agnostic and proudly philosophical; others are emotional in the extreme. If men say that the ethics of Buddhism compare favorably with those of Christ it may be conceded in part, but Buddhism dies at the approach of light. It never vitalized a nation.

QUESTIONS: 1. How many issues and systems does Sir Monier Williams use in describing Buddhism? 2. As regards its founder, how does Buddhism differ from Christianity? 3. As regards sin and suffering, how does Buddhism differ from Christianity? 4. How does Buddhism differ from Christianity as regards God? As regards the future life? As regards love? 5. Explain transmigration, and the doctrine of the karma. 6. When was Buddha born? 7. How often had he been previously born? 8. Whom did he marry? Had he ever before married the same being? 9. How long was he a begging monk? 10. How long did he preach after he received the light? 11. What cardinal point in his teaching is emphasized in his last exhortations? 12. What are the "Four Noble Truths?" 13. What is the "Noble Eight Fold Path?" 14. What is Nirvana? 15. When was Buddhism driven out of India? . 16. What are the leading Buddhist countries? 17 How many sects of Buddhists in Japan? 18. Has Buddhism exalted any nation or people?

CHAPTER XXI.

MOHAMMEDANISM.

1. The Koran is the Bible of above two hundred millions of people. Its teachings are rigidly monotheistic, so rigidly so as to leave no room for an "Only begotten Son" as a days-man betwixt God and man. "There is no God but God," is the oft repeated creed of the Koran. "God is God and Mohammed is his prophet" is constantly on the lips of Mohammedans. In chapter five, entitled, "The Table," it is said, "Christ the son of Mary is no more than an apostle; other apostles have preceded him, and his mother was a woman of veracity; they both ate food." This teaching reduces Jesus to the level of Mohammed, and by necessity destroys the divine authority of his person and revelation.

2. There are 114 chapters or suras in the Koran, and there is no chronological or other order about them, only the longer ones are thrown in first and the shorter ones last. Contradictions are reconciled by the convenient theory that later revelations repeal the enactments of the earlier ones where they happen to be in conflict, but which are earlier and which are later can never be known.

3. The Koran teaches the resurrection of the body with all its passions and appetites. It proclaims an eternal judgment by a relentless judge; it has a sensual heaven and a vicious hell. A perfect harem of black-eyed girls, and rivers and gardens and luxury and lust await the humblest believer who passes from earth. The hell for infidels is literal and terrible, characterized by fire and scalding water and darkness and endless duration. All are infidels who are not Mohammedans.

The Koran teaches foreördination in its most absolute and fatalistic form. The one word *Kismet*, it is fate, settles everything for the Moslem. The effect of this is to make the Mussulman terrible in war; in peace, self-satisfied, and non-progressive.

4. Mohammed seems to have been at first a lofty and serene and sincere soul. He believed in himself, and in his voices and revelations; he preached the unity of God, opposed idolatry, suffered persecution, and lived fondly and chastely with his one wife. Later in life he took the sword, and the persecuted preacher became the merciless soldier. He received revelations in keeping with his temper, hence his divine authority for polygamy and the slaughter of heretics. He per-

mitted his followers to have four wives each; by special revelations he had nine.

5. It is from the last years rather than the earlier ones of Mohammed's life that the Koran gets its character and his followers their example. When the prophet turned soldier he became frantically cruel toward infidels, and represented God as indulging in his own mood. God is merciful, the Koran tells us over and over, but always toward believers, never toward unbelievers. The infidels he will cast into hell. There is no hope for them, since they are predestined to damnation. Over and over in the Koran, war is enjoined upon infidels, and in the chapter entitled "The Cow," believers are commanded to kill the infidels wherever they find them, for it is said, "the temptation to idolatry is more grievous than slaughter."

6. To such teaching is due the horrible slaughter of Armenian Christians in recent years. From the standpoint of the Sultan they were infidels, and they were killed as a religious duty. Judged by the Koran the Mussulman is not a murderer, he is an executioner; he is not a robber, he has a right to his booty; he is not a ravisher, he has a right to his maiden captive, as Mohammed had to Mary the Copt.

7. Mohammedanism has had a wonderful history. It has been a conquering force over vast regions in Asia, Africa, and Europe. In the face of Christian civilization however it is doomed to failure. It has a majestic truth in the oneness of God, inspired by which it destroyed idolatry and united the desert tribes for their great conquests. But it has a mournful error in its rejection of Christ's revelation of God. It knows nothing of the divine Fatherhood, and therefore nothing of human brotherhood. Its fatalism precludes the teaching of repentance and forgiveness, and hence of conversion and redemption. By polygamy it degrades womanhood and puts the harem for the home. The Koran whets the sword, and under the banners of war it sends out the soldier instead of the teacher, the destroyer instead of the benefactor, the slave raider instead of the missionary pastor. It is Christless, loveless, merciless, and fatalistic, but yet as great and rude and rugged as the mountains and simooms of the desert whence it came. With its false Bible this religion comes down through the centuries filling its part of the world with mosques and harems, prayers and massacres, worship and plunder.

8. It is with this religion that our mission-

aries have to deal in Turkey. Many Mohammedans are found also in India and Africa.
The task of their conversion is great, but not
impossible. The home must conquer the
harem, the brother and the democrat must
take the place of the fanatic and the autocrat,
and the broken reed in the hand of the Son of
God must put to shame the smoking sword in
the hand of the presumable prophet of God.
Even Turkey and the Mussulman are included
in the commission, "Go ye into all the world
and preach the Gospel to every creature."
The world's sweet hope lies not in the crescent
but in the cross.

QUESTIONS: 1. How many people embrace Mohammedanism? 2. What is the creed of the Koran?
3. What does the Koran say of Christ? 4. What is
the character of the heaven of the Koran? 5. What
is the meaning of the word Kismet? 6. Mohammed
began as a religious teacher, how did he end? 7.
From which period of his life does the Koran get its
character? 8. What is the attitude of the Koran toward infidels? 9. What effect has this teaching had
on recent history in Armenia? 10. What is the one
great truth of Mohammedanism? 11. Name its
errors as regards (a) Christ; (b) God's Fatherhood;
(c) fatalism; (d) marriage; (e) war; (f) slavery. 12.
In what countries are Mohammedans found other
than Turkey?

APPENDIX.

I. List of Missionaries employed under the direction of the American Christian Missionary Society during the year Oct. 1st, 1897 to Oct. 1st, 1898.

Ainsworth, M. B., Berlin Center, N. D.
Allen, E. W., Buffalo, N. Y.
Allhands, E. S., Arkadelphia, Ark.
Anderson, F. M., Danville, Va.
Bagby, W. H., Salt Lake City, Utah.
Blenus, T. H., Halifax, N. S.
Bolton, R. H., Everett, Mass.
Brazelton, H. J., Anniston, Ala.
Browning, E. C., State Evangelist, Ark.
Burt, D. D., General Evangelist, Neb.
Carnes, Percy T., Lordsburg, N. M.
Clark, Allen G., Muskogee, I. T.
Clark, Geo., Texarkana, Ark.
Cobb, A. P., San Antonio, Tex.
Cook, Scott, Asheville, N. C.
Cowden, W. F., Supt. North West District.
Crockett, W. S., New Whatcom, Wash.
Darst, E. W., Chicago, Ill.
Dotson, C. A., Pendleton, Ore.
Egbert, Jay A., Buffalo, N. Y.
Gates, Errett, Hyde Park Church, Chicago, Ill.
Goodacre, H., State Board, Wis.
Harmon, M. F., Montgomery, Ala.
Harmon, A. D., St. Paul, Minn.
Haston, Jesse B., Galveston, Tex.
Hawkins, S. R., New Orleans, La.
Henry, F. W. S., Gardiner, Me.
Hopper, R. A., Tempe, Ariz.
Humphreys, L. H., Sioux Falls, S. D.
Jenkins, J. W., Hood River, Ore.
Jones, Claude L., State Evangelist, La.

Kellar, E. H., Galveston, Tex.
Lauehart. Frank. State Evangelist, La.
Lingenfelter, B. H., Tacoma, Wash.
Lister, J. B., State Evangelist, Eugene, Ore.
MacLane, H. F., General Evangelist.
McCallum, J. S., Olympia, Wash.
Meyers, W. H., Mobile, Ala.
Mills, Geo., Bangor, Maine.
Mitchell, J. W., State Evangelist, S. C.
Moore, A. R., St. Paul, Minn.
Morris, J. M., General Evangelist, N. Y.
Morrison, G. H., El Paso, Tex.
Nash, W. C., Richmond. Va.
*Neal, Walter A., Jackson, Miss.
Noblitt, T. L., Casselton, N. D.
Northcutt, H. A., General Evangelist, Mo.
Olson, P. S., Hickory, Wis.
Ogburn, Cal., Phœnix, Ariz.
Prewitt, Geo. E., Ponca City, Okla.
Randall, Ed. F., Swampscott, Mass.
Ranshaw, Geo. B., San Antonio, Tex.
Roberts, F. G. S., McAlester, I. T.
Romig, J. A. L., General Evangelist.
Russell, W. J., Kalamazoo, Mich.
Sapp, F. B., Pine Bluff, Ark.
Sargent, Ralph C., Erie, Pa.
Shamhart, W. P., Sioux Falls, S. D.
Sims, G. H., & wife, General Evangelist, Kans.
Small, Jas., Evangelist, Southern California.
Spiegel, J. E., Anniston, Ala.
Smith, J. N., Seattle, Wash.
Stevens, John A., State Evangelist, Miss.
Stevens, R. E., Pictou, N. S.
Stocker, G. C., Johnson City, Tenn.
Tolar, John R., Rochester, N. Y.
Utterback. T. E., Rochester, Minn.
Williams, Virtes, Stillwater, Okla.
*Died.

II.   MISSIONARIES EMPLOYED BY THE C. W. B. M.

JAMAICA.

Kingston, C. E. Randall, 70 Duke Street, Kingston.
M. Isabel McHardy, 70 Duke Street, Kingston.
Berea, P. M. Robinson, Buff Bay, P. O.

Kalorama. A. C. McHardy, Bull Bay, P. O.
Providence, A. W. Meredith, Castleton, P. O.
Oberlin, G. D. Purdy, Lawrence Tavern, O.
King's Gate, Neil MacLeod, Halfway Tree, P. O.

INDIA.

Bilaspur, Central Provinces, Mary Kingsbury.
    "   "   " Ada Boyd.
    "   "   " Bertha F. Lohr.
    "   "   " E. C. L. Miller, M. D.
    "   "   " Lillian B. Miller, M. D.
    "   "   " Mattie W. Burgess.
Mahoba, Northwest Provinces, Mary Graybiel.
    "   "   " Adelaide Gail Frost.
    "   "   " Elsie H. Gordon.
    "   "   " Rosa Lee Oxer, M. D.
Bina Central Provinces, Ben Mitchell, I. M. R'y.
    "   "   " Laura V. Mitchell, I. M. R'y.
    "   "   " Ida Kinsey, I. M. R'y.
    "   "   " Ella M. Maddock.
    "   "   " Ada McNeil, M. D.
Deoghur, Bengal, Jane Wakefield Adam, E. I. R'y.
    "   " Bessie Farrar, E. I. R'y.

MEXICO.

Monterey, M. L. Hoblit.

UNITED STATES.

Montana—Butte, ————————
    " Missoula, J. C. B. Stivers.
    " Deer Lodge, Walter M. Jordan.
    " Bozeman, O. F. McHargue.
Georgia—Athens, W. A. Chastain.
Utah—Ogden.
Oregon—Portland, Chinese Mission, Jeu Hawk
Minnesota—Duluth, Robert Grieve.
Kentucky—Hazel Green, W H. Cord.
    "   "   " Mrs. Wm. H. Cord.
    "   "   " J. South Hawkins.
Virginia—Newport News, W. R. Motley.
North Carolina—Winston, H. C. Bowen.
Arkansas—Little Rock, Evangelist E. C. Browning.
Michigan—Ann Arbor, G. P. Coler.
    "   "   " W. M. Forrest.

III. Names and Addresses of the Missionaries of the Foreign Society.

INDIA.

G. L. Wharton. Hurda, C. P.
Mrs. Emma R. Wharton. Hurda, C. P.
Dr. C. C. Drummond, Hurda, C. P.
Mrs. C. C. Drummond, Hurda, C. P.
Mrs. H. L. Jackson, Hurda, C. P.
Miss Mary Thompson, Hurda, C. P.
Miss Mildred Franklin, Hurda. C. P.
W. E. Rambo, Damoh, C. P.
Mrs. Kate Rambo, Damoh, C. P.
Miss Josepha Franklin, Damoh, C. P.
Miss Stella Franklin, Damoh, C. P.
J. G. McGavran, Damoh, C. P.
Mrs. Helen A. McGavran, Damoh, C. P.
Dr. Mary T. McGavran, Damoh, C. P.
G. W. Coffman, Hurda, C. P.
M. D. Adams, Bilaspur, C. P.
Mrs. Mary D. Adams, Bilaspur, C. P.
David Rioch, Bilaspur, C. P.
Dr. Minnie Rioch, Bilaspur, C. P.
E. M. Gordon, Mungeli, C. P.
Dr. Anna Gordon, Mungeli, C. P.
And twenty-seven native helpers.

CHINA.

F. E. Meigs, Nankin.
Mrs. Mattie R. Meigs, Nankin.
Dr. W. E. Macklin, Nankin.
Mrs. Dorothy DeLaney Macklin, Nankin.
Dr. James Butchart, Lu Cheo fu.
C. B. Titus, Lu Cheo fu.
Mrs. Eunice Titus, Lu Cheo fu.
Dr. Elliott I. Osgood, Lu Cheo fu.
Mrs. Elliott I. Osgood, Lu Cheo fu.
Miss Emma Lyon, Nankin.
Frank Garrett, Nankin.
Mrs. Ethel Garrett, Nankin.
Miss Mary Kelly, Nankin.
Dr. Daisy Macklin, Nankin.
Mrs. Ella C. F. Saw, Nankin.

W. R. Hunt, Chu Cheo.
Mrs. Alice White Hunt, Chu Cheo
Dr. H. G. Welpton, Chu Cheo.
T. J. Arnold, Wuhu.
Mrs. E. Ince Arnold, Wuhu.
C. E. Molland, Wuhu.
Mrs. C. E. Molland, Wuhu.
James Ware, Shanghai.
Mrs. Lillie Ware, Shanghai.
W. P. Bentley, Shanghai.
Mrs. Lillie M. Bentley, Shanghai.
And eight native helpers.

JAPAN.

C. E. Garst, No. 44 Tsukiji, Tokio.
Mrs. Laura Delaney Garst, Tokio.
Miss Kate V. Johnson, Hongo. Tokio.
Frank Marshall, Koishikawa Ku, Tokio
Mrs. Frank Marshall, Koishikawa Ku, Tokio.
Miss Loduska Wirick, Tokio.
E. S. Stevens, Akita, Akita Ken.
Nina A. Stevens, M. D., Akita.
H. H. Guy, Koishikawa Ku, Tokio.
Mrs. Mattie Guy, Koishikawa Ku, Tokio.
Miss Lavenia Oldham, Ushigome, Tokio.
Miss Mary Rioch, Ushigome, Tokio.
M. B. Madden, 18 Soneda, Fukushima.
Mrs. Maude Whitemore Madden, 18 Soneda, Fukushima.
R. L. Pruett, 287 Nishikusabuka Machi, Shizuoka.
Mrs. R. L. Pruett, 287 Nishikusabuka Machi, Shizuoka.
And 27 native helpers.

TURKEY.

G. N. Shishmanian, care of German Imperial Post-office,
Constantinople.
Mrs. Lucy M. Shishmanian, Constantinople.
A. L. Chapman, care of German Imperial Post-office,
Constantinople.
Mrs. Mae Chapman, care of German Imperial Post-office.
Constantinople.
Garabed Kevorkian, M. D., Tocat.
John Johnson, care of British Post-office, Smyrna.
Mrs. Ellen Johnson, care of British Post-office, Smyrna.
And 14 native helpers.

SCANDINAVIA.

A. Holck, M. D., Walkendorfsgade, 22, Copenhagen, Denmark.

R. P. Anderson, Walkendorfsgade, 22, Copenhagen, Denmark.

O. C. Mikkelsen, Slotgate 20, 4 Sal, Copenhagen, Denmark.

Julius Cramer, Malmo, Sweden.

Edvard Nielsen, Christiania, Norway.

Niels Devold, Christiania, Norway

Harold Webster, Fredrikstad, Norway.

A. Johnson, Fredrikshald, Norway.

H. Nevland, Egersund, Norway.

ENGLAND.

W. Durban, No. 43 Park Road, South Tottenham, London W.

Eli Brearley, 5 Reedville, Birkenhead.

E. H. Spring, 26 Worcester St., Gloucester,

H. L. Gow, 2 Park Road, Southampton.

J. H. Bicknell, 38 Newstead Road, Liverpool.

J. H. Versey, 16 Dunbarton Road, Lancaster.

H. A. McKenzie, 65 Everington St., Fuldham, London.

George Rapkin, 2 Myrtle Villas, Margate.

E. M. Todd, 28 Cromwell Grove, West Kensington Park, London.

T. H. Bates, Cheltenham.

AFRICA.

E. E. Faris, Leopoldville, Congo Free State.

Dr. H. N. Biddle, Leopoldville, Congo Free State.